Run With The Wind

Run With The Wind

John Bailey

HODDER AND STOUGHTON
LONDON · SYDNEY · AUCKLAND · TORONTO

My sincere thanks to all who encouraged me with this book. In particular to Dan Wooding, my agent and author of many similar books, Carolyn Armitage, of Hodder and Stoughton, and to Jean Clarke, who typed and retyped the manuscript.

British Library Cataloguing in Publication Data

Bailey, John, 1942, Nov. 1
Run with the wind. —*(Hodder Christian paperback)*
1. Christian Life
I. Title
248.4 BV4501.2

ISBN 0 340 34255 2

 Printed in Great Britain for Hodder and Stoughton Limited, Mill Road, Dunton Green, Sevenoaks, Kent by Hunt Barnard Printing Ltd, Aylesbury, Bucks.
Hodder and Stoughton Editorial Office: 47 Bedford Square, London WC1B 3DP

Contents

To my wife, Jan, who lived it through with me. And to John and Dawn Harris who brought me through it.

'Woe to him who is alone when he falls and has not another to lift him up' (Eccles. 4:10, RSV).

Foreword

Jesus said: 'The wind blows where it wills, and you hear the sound of it, but you do not know whence it comes or whither it goes; so it is with everyone who is born of the Spirit' (John 3:8).

I am very much aware that no one person is ever solely responsible for bringing another to know Jesus Christ as Saviour. Usually, by the time we come to make our own personal commitment to Him, many others have played their part – as well as literature, events, and other means – and all of these have been used by the Holy Spirit to convict us and bring us to a place of repentance and conversion.

None of us knows what part we may have played, by word or deed in bringing others to know him – or, perhaps, in hindering them. But one thing *is* certain. It is the Father, by the power of His Holy Spirit, who brings us all to Jesus.

This book is written to glorify God, not myself, or any other person. Yet, God *has* used people – and many of them – to do that which He purposed for me.

I remember once saying: 'I was running after every wind and whim, doing my own thing. But God waited until I ran out of "pull", then changed the direction of my life by the "wind" of his Holy Spirit. Now I am no longer running *against* the wind, I run *with* the wind.'

God uses us to change the direction of other people's lives, either directly or indirectly, to the degree we allow His Holy Spirit to control *our* lives.

When we forget that we are '. . . not contending against flesh and blood, but against principalities, against the powers, against the world rulers of this present darkness, against the spiritual hosts of wickedness in the heavenly places' we find that our witness is ineffective, and may even hinder the word of the Holy Spirit.

Jesus said: '. . . for apart from me you can do nothing' (John 15:5), which is why He sent the promised Holy Spirit on the day of Pentecost'. Had the apostles been able to bring men and women to Christ by their own efforts, there would have been no outpoured Holy Spirit – and no Church either.

Yet how many of us really give the Holy Spirit the place He seeks in our worship, our praying, and in our witness?

I believe that God is doing a 'new thing' in these last days. He is awakening His slumbering Church and sending out a vast army of laymen, energised by His Holy Spirit, to heal the sick, cast out demons, and work all manner of miracles, as an integral part of the proclamation of the gospel.

This, of course, isn't really a 'new thing' at all. It is simply a restoration and renewal of God's original method of revival: the mobilisation of the masses of ordinary men and women in His Church for the work of the ministry.

This book is about just one of the ordinary people. I do not claim to be a 'special' person, or to possess 'special' gifts, but simply a person who has changed tack in order to 'run with the wind'.

The wind of the Spirit has no denominational anchor, nor can it be contained within any particular doctrinal box, for '. . . the wind blows where it wills, and you hear the sound of it, but you do not know whence it comes or whither it goes . . .'

All we can – and *must* – do is learn how to set our sails so that we 'run with the wind'.

Introduction

I first got involved in working with drug dependents in 1968, more or less by accident. I was walking through the lanes of Brighton, when I came upon a young person crouched up in a doorway. I reached down and spoke to him, and discovered he was chronically addicted to drugs. That encounter changed my whole life and the life of my family. I left my home and my job, and with my wife and young family stepped out in a life of faith to help young drug addicts.

It was on the streets of London that I came into contact with John Bailey. He was one of the countless young people who frequented Piccadilly Circus, the West End and Soho in search of excitement and life, and had been drawn into the web of the drug culture. John had very quickly become a heroin addict and needed vast amounts of money to support his habit. I spoke to him about the claims of Jesus Christ to change and transform his life, and when I see John today I can only stand in amazement. A Christian Minister with a young family, his life is full and free. He is a living testimony to the power of Jesus Christ to transform the human personality.

Run With the Wind, a true story, reminds me of the tremendous interest that Jesus Christ has in the individual. I can only recommend that people read with avid interest what God can do to change lives. John was one of the lucky ones. Many of those early drug dependents with whom my wife, Dawn, and I came into contact, died: some on the streets through overdose, some because they fell in front of vehicles. Some took their own lives through suicide and neglect. John made some attempt to reach out and express that he had a need, a desire to break free from drugs. The book tells the fascinating story of someone who was unimportant in the world's eyes but who was of interest to God.

It has been my privilege to know John, not only as someone to whom I could give support and help, but as a very close friend to my wife and I, almost another son.

Here is a modern day testimony of a young person who, but for the grace of God, would have been just another who faced untimely death, but who through the Lord Jesus Christ has victorious life.

John Harris

Chapter One

Dance In The Rain

It was still dark and raining when we started and at first we worked in the light from the street lamps. I carried bags and cardboard boxes tied up with string out of the house and laid them on the wet pavement while John put them in the boot of the car.

No one else was up. All the curtains were closed and except for the light from the open door the house was dark and looked dismal in the rain.

It was cold, too. John Harris stamped his feet and kept looking at his watch.

Finally, I turned out the hall light, shut the front door and, carrying a small battered suitcase, walked down the path for the last time.

'Okay?' John asked.

'Yeah.'

'Right. Let's get started.'

I threw my suit-case on the back seat and John shut the car boot. We got in. John made no move to start the car.

'Well, what about it?' John asked.

I said nothing. John sighed and shrugged his shoulders.

'Do I have to say it?'

I sat looking straight ahead.

'Okay,' John said. 'You've been smoking.'

The rain rattled on the roof of the car and angled sharply down the windows.

'Why did you do it?' John asked. 'You knew what might happen if you were caught.'

I looked at John.

'Wasn't caught.'

'But you were smoking?'

Silence. John sighed again and started the car.

'Okay. I can't prove it one way or the other. Better leave it at that.'

As we pulled away, John leaned forward, wiped the misted windscreen, then settled back and drove on in silence.

I slumped down in my seat, closed my eyes, and pretended to sleep.

Twenty minutes later we turned into Oxford Street, passed the closed shops and shuttered restaurants, went down Regent Street, through Piccadilly Circus, then turned into a side street, and stopped.

'I've got to get some things from Boots,' John said. 'I'll be about half an hour. That should be long enough to decide what you want to do.'

I looked at John.

'Y'mean y'not throwin' me out?'

John shook his head.

'No. I ought to. But I'm not. You can go and not come back if that's what you want. No hard feelings. You don't owe us. We don't owe you.'

'Or?'

'Or you can take a walk, think it over, and come back in half an hour.'

'Then what?'

'If you come back it means you really want to kick junk,' John said. 'And I'll take you on to Northwick Park. But it's got to be your decision. You have to want it.'

'So who said I don't?'

'I've been in this work long enough to know if a guy is serious or not. You've been totally indifferent to every effort we've made to help you. You've broken rules and you've done everything you can to convince us you're not the kind of young man we want at Northwick Park.'

'Y' sayin' I don't want t'come off?'

'You tell me,' John said. 'You've been on junk, how long is it, eight years? You've been in prison and psychiatric units, and you've had more cold turkey than hot dinners. The fact that nothing worked didn't bother you too much so long as you were always in easy reach of Piccadilly. Now you don't expect anything to work, and you don't want to be stuck in a house in the country miles away from anywhere when you decide it's not working out and you need a fix.'

'So why y'tryin' t'get me t'go?'

John looked at me without speaking, then said: 'You're twenty-eight years old, but you've got the body of an old man. And a sick one at that. If the next fix doesn't kill you, you won't last another winter on the street.'

Outside, the rain poured down. It bounced off the pavement and pools of rainwater that had formed in hollows leaped inches high in the downpour.

'What 'bout my case?' I asked.

'If you don't want to take it, you can leave it with me.'

I opened the car door. John held out his hand.

'Still friends?'

I nodded and shook John's hand.

'God bless you,' John said, 'and remember, if you don't come back and you ever need help, get in touch. Okay?'

I got out of the car.

'Don't worry 'bout me,' I said. 'I dance in t'rain an' run with t'wind.'

Those were the last words my father had spoken to me nearly thirteen years before.

I was fourteen years old and I had stayed out until 2.30 a.m. for the third time in a week. I had not been to school at all that week because my Probation Officer had told the police I was failing to report and they were looking for me.

I threw a handful of gravel at my parents' bedroom window. There was no response. I threw more gravel. Suddenly, the curtain was pulled aside, the window opened, and my father leaned out.

'What t'hell do you want?' he shouted. 'Get out of it. You'll 'ave t'law on us!'

'C'mon, let me in,' I shouted back. 'It's startin' t'rain an' it's cold!'

'That's y'own lookout,' my father shouted. 'You can dance in t'rain an' run with t'wind for all I care, 'cause y'not gettin' in!'

He shut the window and closed the curtains. I shouted a list of purple adjectives, and threw stones at the window, but there was no response.

Ever since the age of eight I had dreamed of going to London to make my fame and fortune as a writer. Now, looking up at my parents' darkened bedroom window, I decided to do it.

I had just enough money in my pocket for a single fare, so I walked the five miles to the railway station, slept in the waiting-room, then climbed aboard the 6.45 a.m. train to London and watched Sheffield vanish in clouds of steam.

'Half an hour,' John called. I shut the car door, and without looking back, walked towards the rear entrance to Piccadilly Underground station.

Inside, I turned left, then right, past the telephone booths in an alcove and the newspaper kiosk, to the stairs at the front entrance to the station.

There were two sets of stairs: one going down into a tunnel that led to the ticket hall, the other went up to the street.

I went down the stairs, through the tunnel, and into the ticket hall. It was crowded with early morning commuters. I pushed through to the next exit tunnel and went into the public lavatory.

There were several vacant toilets. I chose one farthest away from the exit, locked myself in, and waited. When I was sure that no one had followed me I laid my jacket on the damp floor and set out everything I needed – syringe, needles, an empty pill bottle, cigarette filters, and three paper twists of Chinese heroin.

I took off my belt, rolled up my sleeve, then tied the belt

round my arm and pulled it tight. It didn't take long to heat the heroin, filter it, and draw it from the pill bottle into the syringe.

The vein in my arm was up. I eased the needle into the vein, watched as the blood flooded back into the syringe, then slowly squeezed the plunger.

Suddenly, instead of the euphoric sensation I expected, the door and walls started to rush away at tremendous speed. The floor rose up, and I felt myself falling, falling, falling . . .

Chapter Two

A Pat On The Back

Although he had never actually said it I had felt from a very early age that my father hated me. Later I put it down to the fact that he felt trapped in a marriage that wasn't all he had expected it to be. But from the age of five I was very much aware of conflict between my parents and, unlike my sister, who had a more placid nature and was the reason why my father and mother had to get married, I reacted violently.

After my first day at school I refused to go again. Instead, I went for joy-rides on bicycles belonging to children who were in school. Before I was six I was sent to my first children's home as 'beyond parental control'. I was too young to be charged with stealing bicycles, or anything else, so I took full advantage and helped myself to anything that wasn't nailed down.

It was at this time that I discovered the power of putting fear into others. I reacted differently to pain than other children. It started adrenalin pumping into my system culminating in violent rages that left a trail of destruction and injury in my wake.

The staff were reluctant to admit that they were afraid of a seven-year-old, so they shunted me from one children's home to another. I played on their fear, and ruled the other children, some much older than I, as a king who ruled by right of might, until the authorities gave up in despair and almost begged my parents to take me home.

Father wasn't pleased. But, as he had to contribute financially to my being 'in care', he accepted the lesser of two evils and took me home with an assurance that I was now old enough to be charged with criminal offences and, next time, could be sent to approved school free of charge.

Mother always took my side, but she had been arrested for shop-lifting several times, so Father saw us as tarred with the same brush.

Sometimes Mother took my sister and me on her shop-lifting expeditions to keep us out of trouble and as cover for her. Store detectives seemed reluctant to arrest a woman with small children. Usually, they merely retrieved what mother had stolen and gave her a stern warning of dire consequences next time.

It wasn't long before my sister and I went out on our own shop-lifting trips. It was my sister's job to block anyone following me out of the door by falling down in front of them and screaming in agony. Once, a store detective spotted me, stepped over my screaming sister and arrested me. At the hearing in the Magistrate's Court the next day, I thought I heard a rather loud sigh of relief from my father as the magistrate committed me to five years in approved school.

Although it was a tearful good-bye for Mother, I was excited at the prospect of battling my way to the top of the heap again. I felt like the Tar Baby that Brer Rabbit had thrown into the brier patch.

At nine years of age, I was the youngest resident, and the most vicious, at the school. The older boys soon learned that if I lost a fight I could nurse my anger for days, or even weeks, then, when they least expected it, attack them from behind with an iron bar or a brick.

Most of the staff regarded me as potential 'gaol bait' and not worth their time or effort. They were satisfied to keep me 'contained' until it was time for my discharge. That meant giving me the hardest or the dirtiest jobs to do, digging trenches in winter or working in the kitchen in summer. The school was a 500-acre farm. The school staff were also farm staff – the boys were the farm labourers.

I wrote to my mother every week. These letters were always descriptive essays or poetic reflections on my experience at the school. Mother very rarely answered them. Not that I really expected her to reply. She was not much of a letter-writer, or reader either. I wrote them simply as a release valve for my anger and frustration. Occasionally, I wondered what the duty censor made of them.

One day I found out. I was cleaning out a ditch on the edge of a field on a freezing cold day and saw the school English teacher carefully making his way over the frozen ruts towards me. I hadn't seen another human being all day, so I was pleased to see somebody – not that I was going to let him see it!

'Hello, John,' he said when he reached me. I nodded and carried on working.

'Cold enough for you?'

I spat in the ditch, then leaned on the handle of my ditch-tyne and looked at him.

'I thought I'd come over and have a chat,' Mr. Allan said, then put his hand in his overcoat pocket and took out a couple of sheets of paper, 'about this.' He held out the paper for me to see it. It was my last letter to Mother.

'Somethin' wrong w'it?'

Mr. Allan studied part of the letter, then said: 'On the contrary. Let me read some of it . . . "We turned right and entered the park. The trees were close together and the trunks black with rain. Between the trees the lights of cars on the road that circled the park flashed like silent explosions in the distance." ' Mr. Allan stopped reading. I shrugged my shoulders.

'So?'

'Well, that would be pretty good for an adult. But for a ten-year-old . . .'

'Eleven nearly,' I said.

'All right, eleven then. For somebody of that age, this . . .' Mr. Allan waved the letter in the air '. . . is brilliant.'

I looked at Mr. Allan. In the fifteen months I had been at

the school no one had ever given me a pat on the back for anything.

'You seem to have a genuine talent for writing, and a sensitivity of feeling that belies your apparently aggressive exterior . . .'

'What's that supposed t'mean?' I interrupted.

'I'm sorry,' Mr. Allan said. 'What I'm really trying to say is that there is a lot more in you than any of us realise. You have talent, but you have been hiding it under a bushel of anger and resentment.' I said nothing. Mr. Allan looked out across the barren fields then back at me.

'I can help you, John. You have a chance of making something of your life. I would like to help you develop the gift you have. Will you let me?'

I was tongue-tied. Usually, I was told what to do and when to do it. I was never asked to make a decision.

'How?' I asked.

'By letting me introduce you to a world to which you have so far been denied access. Dostoevsky. Tolstoy. Turgenev. Flaubert. Maupassant. Twain. Hemingway.'

I spat on the ground.

'You do like to write?' the teacher asked.

'It's all right.'

Mr. Allan stuffed my letter in his pocket and turned to go.

'Drop in to see me one evening, and we'll take it from there.'

It was a week before I went to see him. Then I started going every week. He loaned me books and set me writing exercises which he tore apart verbally and with a thick red pencil.

'Too wordy, always too wordy,' he said. 'Never use five words if one will do. Remember the three rules of writing. It's simple as ABC. Accuracy. Brevity. Clarity!'

Gradually, Mr. Allan introduced me to Hemingway, then Faulkner, then James Joyce.

'When you can write like this . . .' Mr. Allan handed me Joyce's *Dubliners*. 'The world, and everything in it, will be yours.'

Over the next two years I read, reread and dissected Tolstoy's short stories, Hemingway, Chekhov, and studied their lives, motivations and methods until I felt that I knew them personally.

My own writing improved so much that, once, I fooled Mr. Allan with a pastiche of Hemingway.

'Well done!' Mr. Allan congratulated me, then sighed, 'There isn't much more I can do for you. I'll be leaving the school in a few months. But I want you to promise me to keep at it. You have a unique talent. Use it or lose it.'

'I'm going t'be a writer, Mr. Allan,' I said. 'And I'll put you in my first book.'

After Mr. Allan left the school, things got worse. The other members of staff had disapproved of his 'soft' attitude towards me and came down ever harder on even the slightest infringement of rules. They laughed at my aspirations as a writer and encouraged the other boys to harass me in various ways. One evening I found my copy of *Dubliners* torn in half and the pages scattered on my bed. I exploded and smashed furniture and windows before several members of staff dragged me away and locked me up for three days.

My rages increased in frequency and ferocity. I often beat a boy, or sometimes a member of staff, to unconsciousness. More than once I was threatened with being committed to a mental hospital for the criminally insane.

Mr. Cavandish was a psychiatrist. He visited the school once a month and it was left to him to decide if I was to stay at the school for the remainder of my five years or be sent to a 'special' school for the mentally disturbed.

Mr. Cavandish was friendly, but didn't seem too bright. Since I had been at the school I had done so many I.Q. tests they were now no more than a game that I had learned to play to perfection. The easiest was cards with faces made up with coloured dots. I had to decide which face I liked and which I disliked. As Mr. Cavandish flicked over each card I noticed that he wasn't taking note of which face I had chosen but simply flicked over the card immediately I touched one. It was a game of speed. Obviously it was meant to discover how fast I could make decisions. I touched each card faster than Mr. Cavandish could turn them over. When it was over Mr. Cavandish leaned back in his chair and shook his head.

'In all my years doing this test, I've never seen anyone do it so fast,' he said. 'You can certainly make quick decisions.'

The ink-blob game was almost as easy. So long as I rattled off the most obvious images, and several other more imaginative ones, I scored high marks.

Others were not so easy, so I had to play for time while I worked them out in my head beforehand. One was a complicated jigsaw type puzzle which had to be done within a set time.

I pretended I couldn't understand what was required of me and made Mr. Cavandish go over it again and again while I looked at the different pieces of the puzzle and decided where they had to go.

Finally, I did that one faster than anyone else had ever done it. I worked the same system with drawings of squares, triangles and circles, and having to draw the next figures in the series.

Mr. Cavandish was so excited about my performance he bent the rules slightly and told me what he intended to write in his report.

'Exceptional intelligence,' he said. 'Together with acute perception and a remarkably vivid imagination. The only special school you need is a school for specially gifted children.'

After that there were no more tests. I heard a rumour that Mr. Cavandish was arguing for special privileges for me in study and more creative recreation. But nothing came of it.

Now, I had another weapon. I could convince people that I was much brighter than I really was. I stored it away knowing that some time I would have an opportunity to use it to my advantage.

One day, while I was alone in the big dormitory playing

solitaire, I heard a voice. At first I thought someone had come into the dorm. But no one had. The voice came again.

'The power within you was not given for games,' it said. 'You are not your own. Serve only the power within you and do its bidding.'

I stopped playing cards. The voice seemed to come from within my head. For a moment I thought that perhaps the school authorities were right and that I was crazy.

'No,' the voice answered my unspoken thought, 'but you are chosen. You are the servant of the power within you. Obey it.'

I looked at the cards laid out in a circle on the bed.

'Jack o'hearts,' I said as I touched one, then turned it over. It was the Jack of hearts. I did the same with several others, and got most of them right.

I threw the cards across the dorm. I was scared. The voice in my head started to laugh. I couldn't stop it. I buried my head in my pillow and shouted to drown it out. But the laughter went on and on.

I didn't mention the incident to anyone else. But, a few days later, the voice came back. It began to teach me to do things.

One of the 'tricks' I soon mastered was how to silence a person by saying what he was about to say before he said it.

Another was the ability to 'see' what a particular person was going to do during the course of a day by holding something that belonged to him.

With practice I learned how to do it over even longer periods. But the voice was not pleased with me. Time after time it warned, 'The power within you is not given for games. Serve it. Obey it.'

One morning I had an argument with one of the farm staff. The voice told me to pick up an empty cigarette packet he had thrown away. As I did I 'saw' the man at work on top of a combine harvester. The voice told me to 'see' him slip and get his leg caught by the machinery. Then I was to burn the cigarette packet. I did it out of anger and curiosity. Later that day I saw an ambulance turn into the school gate. The man had slipped on the combine harvester and got his leg mangled in the machinery.

Whether it was a coincidence, or not, I wasn't sure, but the incident scared me so much I 'turned off' the voice by concentrating on something else, anything, when I felt it coming.

On the day of my discharge I was given a smart new suit and a 'licence' that said I had to report to a probation officer once a week for the next six months.

Father was not anxious to have me back home, but, as I was only fourteen and had a court order not to change my address for at least six months, there was not much he could do about it.

Mother was delighted. We celebrated my discharge by going on 'shopping' trips. As my sister was now too old to fall down screaming in front of pursuers, she was the 'lookout' while Mother and I filled our shopping bags.

Although I was supposed to finish my schooling, I didn't go. Neither did I report to my probation officer. As I was out all day and didn't get home very often until the small hours, neither the school authorities nor the probation officer were able to pin me down.

Finally my probation officer alerted the police about my failure to report. They were after me, and the final straw was that fateful night my father locked me out and told me to 'Run with the wind'.

Chapter Three

The Gathering Storm

It was December 10th, 1956, when I stepped off the train from Sheffield at King's Cross. I was fourteen, but looked nearer twenty. I had no money, nowhere to live, and it was bitterly cold.

Apart from Trafalgar Square and the Houses of Parliament, the only other place in London I had ever heard of was Soho. So, asking directions along the way, I walked there.

A cold wind knifed through my thin jacket and jeans. And I was hungry. I hadn't eaten since the evening before, but the excitement of starting a new life in a new place made the cold and hunger seem inconsequential.

Soho was a disappointment. Instead of the colour and excitement I expected, all I found were dirty, narrow streets, market stalls, and unfriendly faces. I wandered about for hours. I didn't know what to do or where to go. By five o'clock I was tired, chilled to the bone, and my stomach was beginning to think my throat had been cut.

The smell of sausages and fried onions started me chatting to a hot-dog seller, hoping he might give me a free sample. He didn't, but, when I told him I had just arrived in London, was looking for a job and somewhere to live, he offered to introduce me to his boss.

The boss was incredibly fat. He was Greek and everyone

called him El Greco as a joke on his massive size, and because his Greek name was virtually unpronounceable.

El Greco owned dozens of hot-dog and hamburger street barrows, and two large dilapidated houses where all his 'boys' lived. He was very enthusiastic about giving me a job and a room, but seemed pointedly uninterested in insurance cards, or why I had come to London without a job and somewhere to live.

It didn't take long to see why. Almost every night El Greco's barrows trundled into the depot crammed with clothes and cheap jewellery stolen from West End stores. It was a twentieth-century Fagin's den, and almost rivalled even Dickens's outrageous inventions, without the sentimentality.

El Greco was a calculating hard-hearted business-man. He paid his 'boys' a third of the marked up price, and invested his profit in an even more lucrative trade, drugs. He bought in bulk, and sold them to his 'boys' at a 'special discount'. Most of El Greco's boys were addicted to something, so what he paid out for stolen goods he got back, and more, by supplying a market he had created.

It suited me. I had a job, a room to write in, and an ambition that provided a door of escape when the time was right. Over the next four years I wrote articles and short stories for women's magazines. I got them all back with a rejection slip neatly pinned to each one.

There were times when my confidence in achieving success as a writer faltered. Periods of chronic depression followed every burst of creative energy. Usually I consoled myself with bouts of heavy drinking or the drugs that El Greco was more than willing to supply.

By the time I had my first short story accepted I was eighteen and already experimenting with heroin. After that first story, everything I wrote was snapped up. I wrote stories and articles on everything from archery to zoology and got them all published in both 'pulp' and 'glossy' magazines.

El Greco was impressed.

Soon, I was able to move out of El Greco's room and

lease a luxury service flat in Edgware Road. Now I could afford to eat in the best restaurants, buy expensive clothes, and throw parties that often lasted all night and usually turned into orgies of drinking, drugs and sex. I rubbed shoulders with the near rich, the near famous, and with those who had once been rich, or famous, but were now merely debauched.

It lasted four years. In order to maintain my life style, and my ever-increasing intake of heroin, I had to turn out articles and stories at a furious pace.

The strain proved too much. Soon I was fixing more often than writing, and what I did write began to come back with alarming regularity.

At first editors were sympathetic. They wrote long friendly letters enquiring after my health. Finally, they stopped writing and started pinning rejection slips to everything I sent them.

My writing career was over. At twenty-two I was a 'has-been'. Not that it bothered me too much. So long as I could find the money to buy the next fix I was happy enough.

Bit by bit I sold everything. Then, when there was nothing left to sell and the rent for my service flat was several months in arrears, I walked out, and joined the other addicts on the back steps of Piccadilly Underground station

Living rough in summer was not too bad. But winter, together with bad diet and heroin adulterated with baking powder or even brick dust, can kill. I saw dozens of addicts die, usually from an overdose but also from exposure and malnutrition.

Over the next six years spells in hospital and psychiatric units together with hepatitis and abscesses that wouldn't heal resulted in long periods of mental problems and a dramatic loss of weight.

During this time many 'do-gooders' came to Piccadilly. Some of them brought soup and sandwiches. Others, 'religious' types, came waving Bibles and 'tracts'.

We tolerated them, and took them for everything we could – money, food, clothes. Sooner or later most of them burned out against our pointed indifference to reform and vanished.

But some persevered. One was Joan. Nothing seemed to dishearten her.

She was young, single, and had an enthusiasm for life that was almost infectious. Although I ridiculed her beliefs and made it clear that she was wasting her time with me, Joan never gave up. She bought me hot drinks and soup in winter and cold drinks and ice cream in summer. We sat on the back steps of Piccadilly Underground station, often all night, and talked. Joan never preached at me or even argued about religion. Sometimes I goaded her and tried to start an argument about the Bible or the Church, but she wouldn't be drawn. I admired her for that and, despite my deliberate antagonism towards her religious belief, I began to feel that if it produced people like Joan then there must be something in Christianity after all.

Then, one bitter winter, I let Joan talk me into getting off the street for a while. She knew a house in Clapham Common that took in drug addicts and alcoholics.

'It's run by a lovely Christian lady,' Joan explained. 'I'm sure I could get you in if you want.'

I agreed, but made it clear that I wasn't interested in getting 'converted', even if it was December, getting colder, and the offer of a warm bed and regular meals for a month or so almost too good to refuse.

Miss Kivistic, or Miss K to the residents, was an old Russian spinster and Mum to the dozen addicts and alcoholics at 16, The Chase.

There were framed Bible texts on the walls and religious 'tracts' and pamphlets on every window-ledge and flat surface in the house. That first night, lying between clean sheets and staring at the Bible verses on the wall, I wondered what I had got myself into.

Joan came every day. She took me for long drives in the country or we spent the day in the park. I began to enjoy not fixing. Joan and I made a game of counting the hours, then the days, since my last fix.

On Sundays Miss K squeezed several of us into her old

car and took us to church.

Although I firmly resisted the religious pressure all around, I noticed a gradual change in me and began to like the idea of getting off drugs for good.

It seemed unlikely. At best I thought I might be able to stay off a few months, until I was fit enough to get back to Piccadilly, but the thought of never fixing again seemed too big a stretch of even my imagination.

One day I was sitting in Miss K's front parlour and feeling bored. There was nothing to read except a pile of religious tracts on a table beside me, so I leaned back and closed my eyes.

I began to think about all the years I had wasted. I was twenty-seven years old. What was the point in trying to kick drugs now? Even if I could there wasn't much of a future for a thirty-year-old ex-addict with a prison record for being in possession of dangerous drugs, who hadn't done an honest day's work in his life.

Suddenly, a voice behind me said, 'John, I've got a plan for your life.' I sat up, startled, and looked round. No one was there.The heavy curtains at the window moved slightly, so I went over and pulled them back, but no one was hiding.

I went back to my chair, my legs trembling, and sat down. 'I'm cracking up,' I told myself and picked up a gospel tract to calm me down. I read, 'For I know the plans I have for you, says the Lord, plans for good and not for evil, to give you a future and a hope.'

'Odd,' I thought, 'that's practically what I just heard.' I dropped the tract, picked up a Bible and opened it at random. There, in the book of Jeremiah, I read exactly the same words. Then I read on, 'Then you will call upon me and come and pray to me, and I will hear you. You will seek me and find me; when you seek me with all your heart, I will be found by you, says the Lord . . .'

'No . . .' I said aloud. 'I don't believe it. God does not exist, it's all in my head.' Then I closed the Bible, and sat waiting. Nothing happened.

'There you go . . .' I told myself. 'It was all in your head!'

But, somehow, I didn't feel very convinced. Somehow this voice was different from the one I had heard at the approved school. That one had been hard, impersonal, and frightening. This one was gentle, warming, and personal. This voice had called me by name.

I didn't mention the experience to anyone. Things were bad enough already. I owed Miss K several weeks' rent and she was dropping frequent allusions to a 'lovely country house in the Cotswolds . . .' called Northwick Park, which I gathered was a rehabilitation centre for drug addicts.

Chapter Four

The Wind And The Rain

One day Miss K called me into her sitting room. In one of the armchairs sat a big man. At first I thought he was a policeman and that Miss K had decided to have me thrown into prison for non-payment of rent or something, but the big man smiled at me.

Miss K introduced me.

'This is Mr. Harris.' The big man stood up and held out his hand.

'Call me John, John.'

'Okay, John, John.' I said facetiously, and shook his hand.

'Well, just John, then.' John laughed and sat down again.

'Mr. Harris wants you to live with him,' Miss K told me.

'Our house is used as the London Centre for Northwick Park,' John explained. 'If you really want to kick the stuff that's where you need to be.'

I said nothing. John looked at me.

'You do want to come off, don't you?'

'What's the alternative?'

John shrugged his shoulders.

'It's January, not a good time for sleeping in the park. Miss K can't keep you indefinitely. Why not give it a try?'

I looked at Miss K. She had her eyes lowered.

'What's this Northwick Park like?'

'Like nothing you've ever seen,' John said. 'It's a big house in the country. You'll like it. It's got lots of trees all around it, and plenty of space to get your head together.'

I shrugged. John was right. It was too cold to sleep out, and, besides, the idea of living in a mansion for a while appealed to me.

'Okay,' I said.

'Fine!' John stood up. 'Just pack a suitcase and we'll get off.'

I looked at Miss K. She smiled at me.

'Go on, hurry, before I cry.'

John lived in the East End, in a fairly small terraced house, with his wife, Dawn, their two-year-old daughter, Rebecca, and six other addicts.

'We're a big family,' John said, 'but we're a Christian family, and that makes all the difference.'

'What difference?'

'Well, for a start, I don't get paid for what we do here and I couldn't support a family this size even if I did, so we have to depend on God to send us the money we need.'

'Oh yeah?'

John let my obvious scepticism pass. The other six residents all seemed to have religious mania. They read Bibles all the time, prayed everywhere, for everything, and out loud.

The worst time was breakfast when John opened the mail and laid a bill on the table. I didn't mind his praying for peace in the world, or missionaries in Africa, but I didn't want to sit there and listen to him pray for God to pay his electricity bill.

'It's stupid,' I announced. 'If you can pray for money like that you wouldn't need wages.'

'I don't get wages,' John reminded me. 'All the money we need we pray for; and it always comes in.'

I could see it wasn't much use to argue with him, so I bowed my head and closed my eyes, while John prayed. When he finished, John folded the bill and put it in his pocket.

'Crazy . . .' I thought, and wondered how soon I could get away from this house.

The next morning John opened an envelope at the breakfast table, then looked at me, smiled and said, 'Thanks, John.'

'What for?' I asked. John handed me a piece of paper. It was a cheque for the exact amount John had prayed for the previous morning. 'Thanks for helping us pray for that,' he said. I shrugged my shoulders and handed back the cheque.

'It would have probably come anyway,' I said. 'It's just a coincidence.'

'Perhaps you're right,' John said. 'But it's odd that when we pray these coincidences happen, and when we don't they stop . . .'

Although I wouldn't admit it, that did seem to be true. Dawn was equally adamant that the whole family should pray for daily necessities – and clothes for her 'boys'.

'Peter needs a new pair of shoes,' she said one day. 'Size eight, black.' Two days later Peter had a pair of shoes – size eight, black.

It was exciting, but I felt out of it. I was as well fed and clothed as all the others. John and Dawn never once made me feel anything other than a real member of the family, but something was missing. Nobody ever sent money or clothes to me *personally*.

'Well,' John told me when I asked him why these things didn't happen for me, 'Maybe it's because you don't ask . . .'.

'Well, if I did, would it happen?' I asked.

'But who would you ask?'

'God,' I said.

'Whose God?' John asked. 'Yours?'

I felt hurt and John knew it. He put his arm round my shoulders.

'Look,' he said gently, 'I can't go and ask Billy Butlin to pay off my debts, but his son can because Billy Butlin is his father, right?' I nodded.

'Well, God answers my requests because He's my father and I'm His son . . .'

'And I'm not, right?' I asked. John shook his head.

'I didn't say that,' he said. 'But if you're not, that's why you don't ask. The Bible says: "We receive from Him whatever we ask, because we keep His commandments and do what pleases Him. And this is His commandment, that we should believe in the name of His Son Jesus Christ." '

'What's that mean?' I asked.

'It means you can't expect anything from God if you won't do what He says and believe in the name of His Son . . .'

'You mean become a Christian?' I asked. John nodded.

'All you have to do is ask . . .' he said. I shook my head.

'No,' I said. 'It's not my scene.'

John didn't press it, but I had to admit to myself there must be something in it. Even a blind man couldn't miss what was happening in that house. Bills *were* being met, money, food and clothes *were* coming in – and all in answer to specific prayer. I wanted to believe it was all pure coincidence. I was afraid what might happen the day I decided it wasn't . . .

I had bad dreams. Three times I dreamt I was on trial for murder. I knew I had done it and, it seemed, so did everyone else, but I argued and protested my innocence despite the evidence against me. Finally, I was found guilty and led down what seemed to be unending dark stairs, growing darker as I went deeper . . .

The words I had heard at Miss K's house, and the Bible verses I had read kept coming back to me, 'Then you will call upon me and pray to me, and I will hear you'.

On Sunday we went to church. After the service the minister shook hands with me at the door, then suddenly asked, 'How is it you haven't become a Christian yet?'

I was stunned. Was this some kind of conspiracy? For the first time in my life I was speechless, then I mumbled 'I don't know.'

The truth was I couldn't think of any logical reason, or even a plausible excuse, why I wasn't a Christian. But I resented being asked in front of a dozen other people and walked away angrily.

Now I was more determined than ever not to give in. It seemed that everyone – including God, if there was one –

was trying to force me into a mould, and I didn't intend to let them do it.

John and Dawn noticed a change for the worse in me. I was rude, avoided anything 'Christian', and smoked less secretly than I had before. Smoking was against the rules of the house, but I hadn't stopped, and now I didn't care if they knew or not.

There were several hints that I might not be allowed to go to Northwick Park.

One evening we had a film in the living room, it was an American 'Christian' film. I sat on the settee with two others, snorting with disgust and grunting all the way through it. When it was over, one of the others on the settee beside me told John he wanted to become a Christian.

While John prayed with him, Dawn looked at me enquiringly. The boy was my best friend, and Dawn's look said, 'See, he's giving his life to the Lord – why don't you?'

It was all too much for me, why couldn't people just leave me alone? I stood up and went to my room, cursing my friend's weakness and determined to beat them all.

That night I had the same dream. I was being tried for murder. But this time I knew that if I did not admit my guilt I should be sent down those dark stairs for ever. Everyone was waiting for me to speak. Just as I was about to open my mouth, I woke up sweating. I was so glad to find myself in bed in that house, and so afraid to go back to sleep, I turned on the bedside light and opened a Bible.

It was the Living Bible and I found myself reading about Jacob. After I had read several chapters I stopped, rubbed my tired eyes, then started again.

'This guy's a crook . . .' I said aloud in surprise. 'And he's in the Bible!' As I read on my amazement grew. I couldn't work out if Jacob was meant to be 'good' or 'bad'. He was a liar, a cheat, and a thief. Yet God had blessed him. I read the account of Jacob wrestling with the angel five times.

It all seemed very familiar. Had I been wrestling with God? Was it even remotely possible that God was interested in me? Did he want to bless me too . . . ?

All the rest of the week I was more subdued. I was thinking. I thought about my past life. I thought about the life that John and Dawn lived, about Joan, about the voice I had heard at Miss K's house – and about Jacob.

John and Dawn left me alone.

The next Sunday we all went to church again. It was full – the church seated about 600 – and everyone was singing as we entered. I sat in a seat some distance away from John and Dawn and the rest, and listened to the singing. It seemed to ebb and flow like a vast sea, then ripple from one side of the church to the other, and I was suddenly caught up in it, lost to everything except the sound and sway of several hundred people singing praises to God. I had never felt so relaxed, so much at peace or almost happy.

Suddenly, I had a vision. At my feet the floor opened up and I saw a long stairway going down and down into darkness. It was the same stairway I had seen in my dream, and I knew I could simply get out of my seat and go down those stairs if I wanted to.

When I looked up I saw the ceiling open and a long bright stairway going up to a bright blue sky. The bottom steps did not reach the floor.

Suddenly the dark stairs were crowded with people, their faces contorted with anger as they pushed and elbowed others out of the way in their almost frantic determination to hurry down the stairs.

There were fewer people on the bright stairs, and much more room. They walked up the stairs, laughing and talking pleasantly to one another.

For one mad moment I wanted to follow the crowd down the dark stairs. Although I could see there was nothing but perpetual darkness down those stairs I felt I wanted to be with the crowd.

Then I looked up again. The bright stairs were empty of people and a dazzling being, shining brighter than the sun, dressed in a white robe tied with a golden sash, stood at the top of the stairs and looked down at me.

'Today you will choose which way you shall go . . .' the dazzling being said. 'You must choose this . . .' he pointed at the bright stairs '. . . or that,' then he pointed to the dark stairs.

'But where are all those people going?' I asked. 'And who are you?'

'You do not know me . . .' the bright being said. 'If you had known me, you would have known my Father also. You will know me and you will also know my Father . . .'

Suddenly, the vision disappeared. I looked around. The singing had stopped and people were sitting quietly or praying. There were several minutes of total silence as if everyone knew that God was in their midst.

I do not remember what the sermon was about, but when the minister finished he asked if everyone would bow their heads and pray while he made an appeal to the unconverted to give their lives to God.

I knew I had to raise my hand, but I didn't. As I looked around the congregation I saw dozens of other people with open eyes too.

'Look at them . . .' I thought. 'These people are supposed to be praying for me, and all they are doing is looking to see who puts their hand up!'

Then, another voice whispered, 'You don't want to join a church like this. These people don't really care about you. It doesn't matter to them if you put your hand up or not.'

'That's right . . .' I thought. 'If they really cared about me they would be praying for me instead of looking about!'

The minister made another appeal.

'I must do it now,' I told myself. Then, the other voice whispered. 'Everybody is looking at you. You'll look silly if you do. What will they think about you when they see you after the service?'

Finally, it was too late. The minister closed the service and everyone started to leave. I sat in my seat wondering what to do. I thought about the two stairways. Had I already chosen one – the wrong one?

'No . . .' I told myself with determination. 'I'm not going to be conned.'

I stood up, went through to the minister's vestry and knocked on the door.

'How do I get saved?' I asked him. 'I want to become a Christian.'

The minister looked surprised, but pleased, and invited me in. He explained the way of salvation very simply and clearly, then asked me if I would like to pray.

'I can't pray,' I said in panic. 'I don't know how . . .'

'Well,' the minister smiled, 'if you just start, I'll carry on for you.'

Nervously, I bowed my head and started to pray. Suddenly, words began to spurt out of my mouth – words of confession, repentance, and commitment. When I finally stopped, the minister looked at me and shook his head in amazement.

'I've never heard such a beautiful prayer . . .' he said, then shook my hand. 'Welcome to the family of God, Brother.'

When I came out of the vestry John threw his arms around me and gave me a bear hug.

'Praise the Lord,' he laughed. 'You know what day this is?' I shook my head.

'Easter Sunday,' he said. 'You couldn't have picked a better day to get saved.'

I smiled. At that instant I knew for sure that God did have a plan for my life. I was aware that it required my willing co-operation, but it was His plan – not mine – and I knew He would reveal it, step by step, in His own time.

After my conversion things seemed to get worse rather than better. I thought now I was a Christian I might fit in better with the family, but nothing I did seemed right.

John and Dawn did their best to guide me in the right direction when it came to reading the Bible and praying, but there wasn't a lot they could do about my relationship with the other addicts. I seemed to rub up everyone the wrong way, even John and Dawn. John had the patience of Job, until he discovered I was sneaking out of the house to smoke.

'You know it's against the rules,' John said gently. 'We can't keep you here, or take you to Northwick Park if you smoke.'

It seemed as if everyone was against me. It had been better when I wasn't a Christian! I began to wonder if I had made a big mistake. I fell into moods of silence, except to make a sarcastic comment, and made it obvious that I had stopped reading my Bible and praying.

Finally, I was openly antagonistic to everything John and Dawn tried to do for me. Any evidence of my new life in Christ almost completely disappeared. Even John and Dawn seemed dubious.

One evening John and I had a big argument. He had smelled smoke on me, but I lied through my teeth insisting that I hadn't been smoking.

'Well, you've not only broken a rule,' John sighed, 'but you seem to be upsetting just about everybody you possibly can. And, on top of all that, you're a liar.'

I said nothing.

'Okay,' John said. 'I want you to pack your suitcase. You can leave first thing tomorrow morning.'

'T'go where?' I asked sarcastically.

'That depends on you,' John said. 'I want the truth. If you can't tell me the truth, how do you expect me to help you? Think it over.'

The next morning John wakened me. It was raining. We ate breakfast in silence, then John indicated the pile of cardboard boxes filled with tins and vegetables, tied up with string, and bags of clothing, all for Northwick Park.

'You can help me put them in the car while you're making up your mind what you want to do.'

Twenty minutes later John stopped the car in the centre of London and gave me my half-hour ultimatum. It looked as if I was back on the street again. Well, I thought as I made my way through the rain to Piccadilly Underground, so much for Christians . . .

Chapter Five

The Fire And The Smoke

Faces floated in the air, coming closer, then drawing away. Someone was talking to me, calling my name. Slowly, my eyes adjusted to the bright lights. I was in bed. There were other beds in rows.

'John, John . . .' a voice repeated my name. 'Wake up, it's me.' Joan's face drifted nearer, wavered, then took on solid shape. I was in a hospital bed with bottles hanging beside it and tubes leading from the bottles attached to my arm.

'You are a very fortunate young man,' Joan scolded. 'They had to punch your chest in the ambulance to get your heart going again. But apart from a few bruises, you're fine.' Joan gently squeezed my hand. I tried to sit up, but a nurse appeared from nowhere and pressed me down.

'Don't try to get up just now,' she smiled. 'We'll get these things away from you in a little while.' Joan clasped her hands and looked at me with mock disappointment.

'What are we going to do with you now?'

'You tell me,' I said.

'I saw John before I came here. He says if you're still willing to give Northwick Park a try, we can forget about this and start again.'

'I'm not sure it's worth it,' I said.

Joan waved her hand around the hospital ward.

'Is this?' she asked. 'At least you'll have somewhere to go when you get out of here.'

There was snow on the window-sill outside and Joan was wearing a thick coat and a woolly hat. She was right. Going back on the street just now would be suicide for me.

'Okay,' I said.

A few days later John drove me to Northwick Park. It was a beautiful 300-year-old mansion less than a mile from the village of Blockley, Gloucestershire.

Frank Wilson with his wife, Shirley, and half a dozen members of their staff looked after twenty addicts. The idea was to take addicts away from the drug scene for six months to a year, instil Christian principles, and help them re-enter normal society as responsible and effective young men.

All residents worked a normal day, had organised activities in the evenings, and relaxed over the weekend except for church services, which were compulsory.

Northwick Park reminded me of every institution I had ever been in. That was the first thing about it I didn't like. The rooms were big, the wood surfaces and doors all highly polished.

One of the addicts, no doubt an 'old boy', pointed at the trail of wet snow I had dragged in.

'Hey, bro,' he frowned. 'Watch where y'walkin'.'

I looked at him stonily. After a long stare he lowered his eyes. Fine, I thought, now we know where we stand.

Although the staff were loving and I was supposed to be a Christian, Northwick Park brought out the worst in me. In every other institution I had to fight my way to the top of the heap, or be used as a doormat, and at the same time let the staff know I couldn't be pushed around. I was used to being a 'top dog', so, when I arrived at Northwick Park I automatically reacted in the same way.

The first bone of contention was the food, which I immediately picked as an excuse for a confrontation. I didn't like spaghetti. At tea on my first day we had spaghetti. When I complained that I couldn't stand spaghetti, I was told, very politely, that spaghetti was that day's menu for tea and there was no other alternative.

'Well,' I began calmly, 'will you find me an alternative? I

can't stand this stuff.'

'I'm sorry,' the girl at the serving hatch insisted, 'we can't just cook you something else because you don't like spaghetti.'

'No.' I raised my voice and shoved the plate of food into her hands. 'In that case you'd better eat it yourself. I won't.'

Then I walked back to my seat and sat at the table with my arms folded. The others said nothing and busied themselves with their own tea. Several minutes later the girl came over and laid a plate of beans on toast in front of me.

'We can make an exception this time, as it's your first day,' she said sweetly. 'But it won't happen again. You have to eat the same as everyone else.'

The girl's name was Rita; she was matron and nurse, and obviously she had done this out of kindness. But, to me, it was a sign of weakness, and I was determined to exploit it to the full.

The next day the same thing happened. This time it was pasty and chips. But the pasty was burned slightly and the chips were cold. In front of about fifty people – residents and staff – I walked over to the serving hatch, laid down the plate, and demanded something else.

'I'm sorry,' Rita said firmly. 'You'll just have to eat what you're given. There's nothing else.'

This time the argument was louder and lasted longer. Rita was adamant. She seemed determined not to give in. Then, Ken, a house parent, came up, smoothed Rita's ruffled feathers, and said I could have something else – this once.

Over the next few weeks I decided I didn't like eggs, salads, any kind of pasta, and a host of other food. When my demands for 'something else' were not met, I ate nothing and sulked.

Now, some of the other residents were starting to complain, not about the food but about me and the apparent preferential treatment I was getting. I soon stopped that with a hard word or a threat of violence – when there wasn't a member of staff in earshot.

People began to look at me oddly. But I just assumed they were becoming wary of me – as I intended. Somehow it never even occurred to me that this wasn't how a professing Christian ought to behave. I was curt, lazy and rebellious.

I avoided work, organised activities and church services as often as I could – and lied when I was asked about it. I soon discovered which residents could be intimidated easily – and which members of staff.

Smoking was strictly prohibited. But I often walked down to the village and bought cigarettes. There was an empty gatekeeper's lodge at the bottom of the long drive and I often went in there to smoke with a friend. His name was Andy. He was hoping to go to university and study for a degree – if he could get a recommendation from Frank Wilson. But he had one fatal weakness – as a Christian he found it difficult, unlike me, to tell a lie.

One day someone saw us heading for the empty lodge together and suspected we were smoking. The next day we were called into the office by John Dean, a house parent, and questioned separately about it. Andy went in first and admitted he had been smoking. This was a serious breach of rules and often resulted in the culprit's being 'asked to leave' – a euphemism for getting thrown out. But, as Frank Wilson was away in America on a fund-raising tour – which he seemed to be most of the time – Andy was told he would have to wait until Frank Wilson returned.

I went in next. John Dean's weakness was his willingness to believe the best – even about someone like me – and he wanted to give me the benefit of whatever little doubt there was about my guilt. I said no, I hadn't been smoking.

'But you were with Andy?' John Dean asked.

'Yes,' I said. 'I wanted to help him get over whatever problem was making him smoke.' John Dean swallowed it well, and smiled at me.

'That's wonderful,' he said. 'A really Christian thing to do.'

Then he went on for the next ten minutes telling me how

well I must be coming along if I was doing that kind of thing – and in secret, too! Finally he promised to make a note of my charitable act and mention it to Frank Wilson when he got back.

Unfortunately, Andy couldn't take the strain of waiting, and left before Frank returned. I didn't feel bad about helping Andy to ruin his chance of going to university. I was happy I had managed to turn the situation so nicely to my advantage, and pleased that Andy was no longer around to spill the beans when Frank came back.

But I didn't fool everybody. Rita and her friend Jan – who looked after the married staff's children – were sure I was smoking, but could not prove it.

The first time I saw Jan I liked her. One day Andy and I were standing at the top of the main stairs when Jan walked by below.

'That's a nice girl,' Andy commented. Almost without thinking words popped into my head.

'I'm going to marry her,' I said. Andy looked at me, then laughed.

'You?' he asked. 'She would never marry you.'

'No?' I asked, a strange certainty taking hold of me. 'I'm telling you. One day I'm going to marry that girl.'

On reflection it seemed impossible. Jan came from a Scottish Baptist background – very strait-laced. On top of that any romantic relationship between residents and members of staff was strictly forbidden. An addict, it was said, could not handle romantic involvement and kick drugs at the same time. The staff were supposed to be mature enough to recognise and avoid the danger. If not, the girl rather than the addict – who might go back on drugs – had to leave.

Apart from all this, Jan didn't even like me.

I used every opportunity to talk to her, or be where she was. The one thing I found I could not do was flatter her. I used flattery on most of the other single girls – and some of the married ones – to smooth away any suspicions they had about me and to make them less ready to report these suspicions to Frank. After all, he might suppose there was something between us and suggest the girl should leave!

I didn't want that to happen to Jan, so my attentions were more subtle. Nevertheless, Jan did her best to avoid me.

During this time my increasing bad behaviour was causing grave concern. I was threatened, more than once, with being asked to leave if my behaviour and attitude did not improve.

Although I never admitted it I was getting concerned too. I didn't understand myself. As a Christian I knew I ought to be different from what I was before. I couldn't seem to stop myself doing the worst, even though, inside, I really wanted the best.

As far as I, or anyone else, could see, the only difference being a Christian had made in my life was that I no longer swore – little enough result of the supposedly transforming power of Jesus Christ! Many people came to the conclusion I hadn't really been 'born again', and I was no longer sure.

I read my Bible, prayed, and studied other Christian books, as much as anyone. I knew I'd had a wonderful 'experience' in the church in London and that my prayer asking Jesus into my heart and life had been sincere. Yet it had not seemed to have changed me at all.

Things were so bad with me that when I added my name to a list of those who wanted to be baptised in water it was tactfully suggested that perhaps it might be better if I withdrew my name!

But I did not. I was so angry that anyone dare suggest I was too bad to be baptised in water I insisted on going – and go I did.

The service was in a Baptist church in a town a few miles away from Northwick Park. I sat on the front row with several others to be baptised and looked at the girl playing the piano. She had lovely legs and wore the shortest mini-skirt I had ever seen. Even while I was looking I knew my thoughts were hardly suitable for such an occasion, and I finally admitted to myself that I probably wasn't a real Christian at all.

I watched dejectedly as each one testified, then was baptised, as I waited my turn. I considered walking out of the church, but before I had made up my mind my name was called.

The water was cold as I stepped down into the baptistry. As I went down I inwardly told God He ought to have allowed me to die from a drug overdose or even a road accident than let me do this. Had I known what little difference it would make in my life by receiving Christ, I told Him, I would never have done it. I hoped I would have a heart attack, or drown under the water.

Then, splash! I was under, then out. As I stood up and put my foot on the first step of the baptistry, I turned and looked down at the water. I saw my own reflection, distorted and broken up in the swirling water. Suddenly I knew that something wonderful had happened. That body under the water was me – or rather the old John Bailey. He hadn't got out after all! He *had* died under the water – and I was a new creature born out of the old.

In the coach on the way back to Northwick Park everything suddenly looked new – the flowers, the trees, the fields. I was astonished, and hurt as I listened to the jokes and chatter of the others who had just been baptised. How could they take so lightly what they had just done, I wondered? Then the Lord rebuked me for my unloving attitude towards them, and I spent the rest of the journey back inwardly rejoicing in the Lord and praising God.

From then on there was a dramatic and definite change in my attitude and behaviour. Everyone noticed it. There was now no longer any doubt in my mind and heart and I really was a Christian. The Bible took on a new meaning for me. For weeks I could not read anything else. Finally, I knew that God had shown me the next step – Bible College.

In the natural way it was unlikely. I had little formal schooling – most of my school days had been spent running away from school – and at thirty-one years of age, I wasn't sure if I could cope with serious academic study. Also, I would need money, or a grant, and no idea how I, with such a bad work record, would ever get it. But I knew that God had said it. And I knew that what God has said He will also do!

The other problem was Jan. Since my baptism I had felt a deep assurance that she was the girl God intended to be my wife. But so far there had been little apparent change in her attitude towards me.

Then, suddenly, the worst possible thing happened. Jan decided she would rather work with girls instead of boys and was leaving Northwick Park! How could this be, I asked the Lord? If she left now it was almost certain I should never find her again.

The morning Jan was leaving I kept out of the way. It was possible that she might change her mind even yet, I told myself. I watched from a window as she shook hands and said good-bye to her friends. I was shattered. I could not bring myself to go down and say good-bye.

As she got in a friend's car, and it went down the drive, I looked up and said, 'Well, Lord, you've really got to work a miracle this time.'

Then I went upstairs to my room, determined to leave Northwick Park as soon as I could.

About a month later Frank Wilson called me into his office and asked me if I would like to work in the Billy Graham Evangelistic Association office in London. Apparently Frank had originally made enquiries on behalf of Andy, and had forgotten to cancel the application – confusing me with Andy. So would I like to take the job instead?

'When do I start?' I asked.

'First thing on Monday morning,' Frank said. Today was Thursday.

'When can I leave?' I asked.

'Tomorrow,' Frank said.

'Okay,' I said. 'I'll take it.'

Friday morning I threw my suitcase on the back seat of the car that was to take me to the railway station and got in. I didn't say very much on the way to the station. I was too busy thinking. I was leaving Northwick Park at last. But I was now a different person from the one who had arrived eight months ago.

Chapter Six

A Second Blessing

After leaving Northwick Park I went to live with John and Dawn Harris again. I started work at the Billy Graham Evangelistic Association office and dreamed about going to Bible College. I still didn't know how it was ever going to come about, but I was certain it would.

I went to church several times a week attending every Bible study, prayer meeting and missionary evening – even though it took over an hour to get there. For the first time in my life I felt really alive, really free and overflowing with real joy and inner peace.

The people at the office commented on it, and soon everyone had heard my testimony.

But there was one thing that still bothered me. I hadn't been able to give up smoking, and I couldn't understand it. I had prayed about it, and believed that the Lord would take away the desire, but it had not happened.

I marvelled at how the Lord had so completely delivered me from the bondage of heroin addiction. That was a miracle almost beyond belief. I was awed that He had made me His child, no more a child of the devil. That constantly amazed me. I was thrilled that God had a plan for my life and wanted to use me. That excited me. So why couldn't I give up smoking? What was I doing wrong?

One day I heard about a man who had a ministry of deliverance and decided to go to one of his meetings and ask for prayer for victory over the habit.

The friend who took me was a member of this man's church and warned me that I might find the service a little noisier than I was used to. He was right. The mainly coloured congregation sang the same chorus for over twenty minutes – standing on the seats and running around the church as they sang – then sang another for a further twenty minutes.

When the white minister finally opened the meeting, several people swooned in an aisle and had to be helped out. I didn't like it. Although I belonged to a Pentecostal church, this was really too much. But, if I was going to get victory over my habit, I was willing to suffer through this service.

There was another hour of chorus singing, running around the church, and dancing on the seats, then the minister started to preach. He spoke about the power of Jesus over the power of the devil, and mentioned specific examples: drug addiction, alcoholism, and smoking. My ears pricked up when he related instances of miraculous deliverance from such bondages.

When he finished he made an impassioned appeal to the unconverted to receive Christ as Lord and Saviour. Then he made it again, and again. Remembering my own experience, when I saw people idly looking around the church while the appeal was being made, I kept my eyes closed and so didn't see if any put their hands up.

Then the minister asked those who wanted deliverance from some habit to raise their hands. I put my hand up, still keeping my eyes closed, then lowered it. After a general prayer of thanksgiving the minister called for the young man in the black suit and blue tie to step forward. I looked up. The minister beckoned to me. It seemed I was the only one who had raised a hand for deliverance – so I went forward.

Immediately, the man gripped my head with both his hands and started to ask the Lord to save this young man's soul. I whispered that I was already a Christian and wanted deliverance from smoking, but the man was so busy pleading with the Lord to save me, he didn't hear. I tried again, a little louder, but he was now in full flow and would not be stopped.

Suddenly, he pressed his hands harder on my head and commanded me to confess my sins and receive Jesus Christ as my personal Saviour. 'I am saved,' I hissed at him, 'I'm already a Christian.'

The minister must have assumed I was a reluctant unredeemed sinner, and would not be put off.

'Confess,' he commanded. 'Confess your sins and receive Jesus Christ as your personal Saviour.' I tried once more.

'But I am saved. I just came for deliverance.'

But the man almost shook my head off my shoulders and cried: 'Don't give way to the devil, confess your sins and receive Christ Jesus.'

Reluctantly, I gave in, made a prayer of confession, and asked Christ into my life – for the second time. The congregation, almost as one man, gave a sigh of relief and started shouting 'Hallelujah' and 'Praise the Lord' and 'Thank you Jesus'.

When it was all over and people were starting to leave I walked over to the minister and explained his mistake. 'You see,' I told him, 'it was a smoking problem I came about, not my soul.'

The minister shrugged his shoulders.

'Oh well . . .' he said, 'never mind.'

'But what about my smoking problem?' I asked.

'Oh, don't worry about that, son,' he said, 'just give it up . . .' Then he turned and walked away.

On the way home I looked up at the night sky and said, 'Lord, this smoking habit might kill me. But if it does I certainly know where I'll spend the rest of eternity. You've saved me twice now.'

Although the incident was funny, on the way home I received a quiet assurance that there were many more important things in the Christian life than not smoking. And, after all, the preacher *was* right. If I really wanted to stop smoking, all I had to do was give it up.

That night I went to bed with a lot more self-understanding, and a little wiser.

In those first few weeks after leaving Northwick Park, I learned a great deal about prayer from John and Dawn Harris. I was fortunate to be living with a couple who had a special interest in the practical application of prayer to everyday life.

Prayer, to them, was not only a form of worship, a Christian duty, and public confession. It was a matter of urgent need. It was their daily bread. And as such there was no place in it for flowery speeches or pious phrases. Their prayers went straight to the point of their need – whether that need was great or small. John's and Dawn's practical example taught me that my Father delights in giving to His children and that praise and worship are the fruit of thankfulness for His provision.

But not everyone I knew thought the same.

A minister friend and I once visited an old Christian couple who had absolutely nothing in the way of material goods. There was no electricity in the house and the wallpaper was falling off the wall in places owing to damp. This old couple often spent their day huddled in blankets to save heat. They ate frugally and never went out except to church on Sundays. They prayed, read their Bible, and suffered their poverty with stoic resignation.

My minister friend immediately asked them why they were living in such a terrible condition as they were both children of the Father and therefore heirs to all His promises of abundance.

They explained that although they were poor in 'material' possessions, they were 'spiritually' rich. My minister friend talked to them for over an hour and in all that time there was not one 'Hallelujah' or 'Praise the Lord'.

They were 'pious', but completely negative, and harboured bitterness and resentment against almost everyone. Despite their 'spiritual' riches, there was neither joy nor love in their hearts.

Before we left my minister friend suggested that the old couple should confess their bitterness and resentment and ask the Lord for some specific material gift. They refused. They had been told it was wrong to ask for material things, so they never did.

We left, after prayer, and the minister commented, 'Whatever the theological arguments you get into about praying for material things, always remember this old couple – they neither ask, nor do they receive.'

I made a habit of taking my Bible to the office so that I could read it on the train. One day the Lord showed me how it might go with me unless I was always careful to apply what I read to my daily life.

An old man who had been watching me reading my Bible finally came over and sat beside me.

'Take the advice of an old fool,' the man said. 'Be sure to do everything in that book, whatever it costs. I didn't and my whole life has been wasted and ruined because of it.'

Then he told me his story. Apparently, as a young man, he had given his life to the Lord and, for a time, all went well. But then certain passions condemned by the Word of God so gripped him that soon his spiritual life drained away.

'My whole life has been wasted when it could have been mightily used in God's service,' he concluded. 'And the tragedy is that the passions that ruled my life for so long and laid it waste no longer interest me now that I am old.'

Tears ran down his face as he said, 'Remember, obey the Word of God – resist the devil and he will flee from you.' Then he gave me a Bible reference to look up. It was 1 John 2: 17. 'And the world passes away, and the lust of it, but he who does the will of God abides for ever.'

That incident had such a profound effect on my heart I made a vow to the Lord right there and then that, with His help, I would live my life with the old man's face ever before me and his story engraved on my heart.

Despite all I was learning at John's and Dawn's, and enjoying working at the Billy Graham Evangelistic Association office and being involved in church activities, I had not forgotten Jan.

It seemed impossible we should ever meet again. No one

knew what had happened to her or even to which city or town she might have gone.

'Pray . . .' John insisted. 'If it's right you'll meet.'

So I prayed – and made enquiries. But nothing came of it. I just couldn't understand. I was absolutely sure that Jan was the wife God intended for me.

'You could be wrong,' John told me. 'There are other Christian girls, you know.'

He was right. There were other Christian girls – some right in the office where I worked. But I felt I was already married to Jan – it was just that she wasn't around at the moment.

One Sunday morning after the service I was standing outside the church talking to John and some other friends. It was hot, the church had been full, and I was tired and ready to go home.

I glanced at a crowd of people coming out of the church – and my heart jumped a beat. I rubbed my eyes and looked again. It was impossible . . . but yes . . . it was Jan.

She saw me, and smiled. Then she walked down the church steps and made her way through the crowd.

'Hello, John,' she said. 'It's nice to see you again.'

'Yes, it is . . .' I said, and laughed until everyone thought the sun had affected me.

'All right now?' John winked at me.

'Fine,' I smiled. 'Everything is just fine!' I could hardly believe this was happening.

'I'm speaking at the Richmond Baptist church on drug addiction tonight,' Jan said. 'Would you give your testimony?'

Everything seemed to be working together.

'Yes,' I said immediately. 'I'd love to.'

'Lovely,' Jan smiled. 'I'm living at St. John's Wood so we had better meet at Notting Hill Gate tube station at six o'clock.'

'Fine,' I said.

'But don't be late,' Jan warned. 'There aren't many trains to Richmond on Sundays.'

'Don't worry,' I laughed. 'I'll be there.'

Chapter Seven

A Kiss In The Dark

All that afternoon I was walking on air. The impossible had happened. Now I was sure that God had all things in His hand even though I couldn't see how, and all I needed to do was to wait on Him.

In the bath I started to worry a little. Perhaps I had been too hasty in agreeing to go to Richmond Baptist church and give my testimony. Public speaking terrified me. Usually I went dumb in front of an audience, or started to sweat or both.

But Jan's invitation really did seem a godsend and, besides, this time it might be different. Surely, if God could work it so that Jan and I got together again – an absolute miracle in itself – then He could also bring me through this.

It was important that Jan should be impressed with my performance at Richmond that night. I was sure that God understood, and would make sure all went well for me. Although I was in love with Jan and I knew she was the girl God intended as my wife – she was not yet in love with me. I needed everything to go well tonight so that she would agree to go out with me again – and again.

I arrived at the tube station late. I had waited almost an hour for a bus that didn't come, then jumped into a taxi and got there late.

Jan greeted me politely, and looked at her watch.

'Sorry I'm late . . .' I said.

'We should make the connection at Earl's Court all right,' she said. 'But if we miss it, we won't get there.'

I could see she was annoyed. On the train I looked at Jan's reflection in the window on the opposite side and said nothing. My acute embarrassment in being late and getting Jan annoyed had dried up all the witty and charming things I had planned to say to her on the long journey to Richmond. It wasn't a very good start.

At Earl's Court we almost missed the train. It was pulling out a minute or so early and we had to run to catch it. Jan sat on the train looking straight ahead. I sat beside her in silence.

As each station went by I promised myself I would say something to her before the next one. But I didn't. 'I'll ask her for a date on the way back to the station after the service,' I told myself.

The church hall was packed full. I hadn't expected such a crowd. While Jan was speaking I looked out over the sea of curious faces and felt my courage evaporate. My hands began to sweat, my stomach was in knots and my throat felt like a rasp.

Suddenly Jan introduced me. I stood to my feet and stared dumbly at the congregation. Sweat prickled my brow as I launched myself into my testimony. I was more aware of the pained expression on people's faces than what I was saying.

'O Lord,' I thought as I rambled on, 'what are you doing to me?'

Now sweat poured down my face in rivulets. People coughed and shuffled their feet uncomfortably. Some even looked away in embarrassment.

When it was all over and we were sitting drinking coffee, the youth leader who had invited Jan, came over, looked at me in amazement and said,

'I've never seen anyone sweat so much. You were really in a state!'

Jan said nothing.

We left as soon as was decently possible and arrived at

Richmond station twenty minutes early. I didn't know what to say. I mumbled an apology for ruining her evening. Then we waited for the train in silence.

Back at Earl's Court, we had to wait for the train to Notting Hill Gate.

'Watch the boards,' a porter told us. 'Should be one along in about twenty minutes.'

Trains came in, and went out. But ours didn't appear on the illuminated boards. Jan shivered with the cold.

'What time is it?' I asked, hoping to start a conversation. Jan looked at her watch.

'Eleven o'clock,' she said.

Other trains came in, and went out. Now, the trains were less frequent. Suddenly, I realised we had not seen any for some time. And there was still no sign of ours on the boards.

'What time is it?' I asked again. Jan looked at her watch.

'Eleven o'clock . . .' she said, then put the watch to her ear, and groaned. 'Oh no,' she said, 'it's stopped.'

I looked for the station clock. It said five minutes to twelve. Jan was close to tears.

'What are we going to do?' she asked. I tried to put my arm around her to comfort her, but she moved away.

'I'm sorry,' I said. Jan said nothing. A porter came along the platform pushing a broom. I asked him if there were any other trains we could get.

'Trains?' He laughed and pulled out his pocket watch. 'It's midnight. Trains all stopped half an hour ago. You shouldn't even be in the station. Better get out before you get locked in for the night.'

He watched us as we went up the stairs and out to the street. Outside all the buses had stopped, too. And we didn't have enough money between us for a taxi.

'What are we going to do?' Jan moaned. 'It's miles to St. John's Wood.' She was right. It would take hours to get back. The situation didn't look good.

'We'll just have to walk,' I said. Jan looked at me wide-eyed.

'Walk?' she asked. 'I can't walk all that way!'

I was getting angry.

'Well we can't stand here all night,' I said, and took her arm and propelled her along the street.

Every hundred yards or so Jan wanted to sit down, but I dragged her along.

'Maybe God is trying to tell you something,' I said. 'Us being alone together like this.'

Jan stopped and looked at me.

'He's not trying to tell me anything!' she snapped, then walked on a little faster.

At Hyde Park Corner, Jan collapsed on a seat and refused to go on.

'It's no use, I just can't go any further,' she groaned. I looked at her. She was tired, so I sat beside her and put my arm around her shoulders. This time she didn't move away.

'I'm sorry,' I said. 'It's all my fault. If I hadn't tried to impress you all this wouldn't have happened.'

Jan looked up at me with tears forming in her eyes.

'Is that what happened?' she asked. I nodded and we sat together without speaking.

'Would you consider going out with me some time?' I whispered. 'A date, I mean?'

Jan sighed and shrugged her shoulders. 'That depends where and when,' she said.

I thought quickly. I knew she liked classical music and opera, and I remembered seeing an advertisement for Elizabeth Schwarzkopf at the Royal Festival Hall. I didn't have any tickets and I knew such an event would be booked up months in advance. But I knew it was an offer Jan couldn't refuse. A plan was already forming in my mind.

'How about tomorrow night?' I asked. 'Elizabeth Schwarzkopf is at the Royal Festival Hall.'

Jan looked at me incredulously.

'Elizabeth Schwarzkopf,' she said delightedly. 'Have you got tickets?'

'No,' I beamed, 'but I can get them. What about it?'

'All right,' Jan smiled. 'It's a date.'

I finally got Jan back to Maida Vale, said a polite 'good-night' and started the long walk back to the East End. It took me another two hours and I didn't get back until four o'clock. But the journey seemed only a few minutes. I was walking on air. Besides I needed time to figure out how I was going to get two tickets for that night.

At breakfast that morning John was not happy with me.

'What do you mean by coming home at four o'clock in the morning?' he said. 'We're not running a hotel you know.'

I explained everything in great detail, but John didn't seem convinced.

'Are you telling me you didn't get Jan home until two o'clock?' he persisted. 'And you walked from St. John's Wood?'

I nodded resignedly. It seemed incredible I knew, and having so recently come off drugs, I couldn't blame John for being suspicious. But what else could I say? John finished his breakfast in silence.

Fortunately I was on flexi-time at the Billy Graham office, and I had a few hours in hand so I worked that morning and had the afternoon off. I went down to the Royal Festival Hall and tried to buy tickets at the booking office for the performance that evening.

'Sorry,' the ticket girl told me. 'All the tickets for Elizabeth Schwarzkopf were sold out weeks ago.'

I was disappointed but not surprised. I sat on a seat and wondered what to do. There must be a way a bright young man like me could get tickets, I thought.

I wandered around the reception hall all afternoon, watching and keeping my ears open. At about four o'clock a man and woman came in, quarrelling loudly. I saw the two tickets the man was waving in the air. It seemed, he wanted to hear Elizabeth Schwarzkopf that evening and she did not.

After a few minutes I walked over to them and said, 'Excuse me, I couldn't help overhearing your problem. Perhaps I can help . . .'

'What do you mean, help?' the man asked suspiciously. I quickly explained my problem to him, then said, 'How much did those tickets cost you?'

'Two pounds fifty each,' he said.

'I'll give you twelve pounds for both of them,' I offered. 'It's that important to me. And you can have a much better evening on twelve pounds that you can on five.'

The man looked doubtful, but the woman encouraged him to accept my offer.

'All right,' the man said at last. 'Done!'

I felt ten feet tall as I walked away from the Royal Festival Hall with my prize.

It was a wonderful evening. Jan looked lovely, Elizabeth Schwarzkopf was good, and it seemed as if everything was going to work out fine. At the interval we had coffee and talked.

I told Jan about my plans for the future. 'Bible College,' I said. 'God says I'm to go to Bible College.'

'How can you be so sure?' Jan asked kindly. I was tempted to tell her I knew because she was there with me tonight, all part of God's plan for our lives together. But I didn't. Instead, I said simply,

'I just know.'

After the concert we had a meal, then I took Jan home. She worked as a nanny in a big house and when we reached the gate, Jan said,

'Thank you, this will do fine.'

I nodded and looked at her.

'It's been a lovely evening,' she said. 'I don't have much time to go out a lot, so this evening was really special. Thank you.'

Jan held out her hand.

'Would you be offended if I kissed you?' I asked, and before she could answer I took her in my arms and kissed her on the lips. It lasted a long time. Then Jan broke away, murmured an embarrassed goodnight and hurried through the gate and up the long drive.

All the way home I was rejoicing. I knew something had happened when I kissed her – something in her. I had felt a softening – nothing I could put into words, but a definite change in her attitude towards me. This was God at work, I felt sure. And what He had begun He would also bring to completion.

I didn't see Jan again for several days. In the excitement of the moment I had forgotten to ask her out again, so I telephoned, and she said, 'Yes'.

After that we started going to Bible study evenings and prayer meetings together. John and Dawn seemed pleased, I was happy, but Jan was cautious. One evening, on the way home after a Bible study, I asked her,

'Could we start going out together – on a regular basis, I mean?'

Jan looked at me shyly.

'We'll see,' she said. 'We'll see.'

Chapter Eight

The Wind Of The Spirit

From the very start the relationship between Jan and I was flinty. I still had a great many problems. I was very abrupt with people or retired into a 'mood' if I couldn't get her away from her friends. I was rude to people who tried to patronise either of us because I thought they were wondering why a nice Christian girl like Jan wanted to get mixed up with an ex-addict. I felt they looked down on me, and were sorry for Jan.

All my pre-Christian contempt for 'straights' re-emerged in defence of Jan's relationship with me. I was very much in love with her and I wasn't going to allow anyone who didn't know anything about life – by life I meant the kind I had lived before my conversion – to pass judgment and condemn our relationship.

I was very critical of the seemingly low level of spirituality of other Christians without realising that my own attitude and behaviour were becoming increasingly worse than anything I was complaining about.

Jan and I even quarrelled about it.

'But what about your attitude?' she asked.

We were sitting in a café an hour before the Sunday morning service was due to start and we were almost at one another's throats.

'My attitude!' I shouted, and thumped the table. 'I'm the

one that's got the problems. What do they know about life? Most of them have been Christians all their lives. What problems have they got? I've only just started. I'm the one who's got problems. They've got it easy compared to me!'

Jan shook her head.

'That's no excuse' she said, 'If Jesus has changed you and lives within, you should be working to make that change apparent.'

'But what about them?' I protested 'They haven't got a problem in the world, and they still can't go on with God. They whimper about this, whine about that. They say they find it hard to pray, or hard to read their Bibles. How come I can do all these things and they can't? I'm the one that's got all the problems.'

At that point a waiter came over and asked if we would like to order. Jan ordered a coffee. 'Apple pie and ice cream,' I said curtly. The waiter shook his head.

'I'm sorry sir,' he said politely. 'We are only serving breakfast at this time.'

I stared hard at the man.

'That is my breakfast,' I snapped at him. Jan lowered her head in embarrassment. The waiter went away and brought back a plate of apple pie and ice cream.

'I don't know.' Jan seemed close to tears. 'I just don't understand why you act like this sometimes. Some of my friends are beginning to think you're not really a Christian at all.'

That shook me. It sounded familiar. But I was the one who was complaining that others were living un-Christ-like lives. There was nothing wrong with me. It was them.

The last thing I wanted to do was hurt Jan. It was just that she seemed to be blind to other people's faults and even suggested the faults I saw in others were really my own! Usually, we made up very quickly, and then tried to avoid certain subjects for a while.

It was Dawn who made me see that perhaps Jan was right. I was helping her wash up and commented about a man in the church. 'Oh, he's just got a chip on his shoulder.' Dawn laughed and nudged me in the ribs.

'He has . . .?' she asked. 'Look who's talking.'

'What do y'mean?' I asked her.

'You've got a chip on your shoulder the size of Buckingham Palace.'

I was taken aback. Then I decided Dawn was joking.

'Come on, Dawn,' I laughed. 'I'm a new creature in Christ. All that's behind me now.'

'You're kidding yourself,' Dawn said seriously. 'What's all this nobody-loves-me stuff? Nobody has got problems except you? Poor me . . .' Dawn mimicked. 'I'm an ex-junky. I can't be expected to be nice to other people, to help them. They all ought to be helping me.'

'Steady on, Dawn,' I said. 'I'm not as bad as all that!'

Dawn looked annoyed.

'No?' she asked. 'Do you know I've seen that girl of yours in tears over how you behave in public sometimes. She's a lovely girl. If you're not careful you could lose her.'

That made me think. For the next few weeks I made a special effort to be 'nice' to other people when I was out with Jan. I took pride in the fact that I let people get away with saying daft things, or moaning about their problems.

When we were alone we prayed together more, and studied the Bible. When we were apart we arranged to read a passage of scripture at a particular time.

But, before long, I exploded again. Sometimes we quarrelled so badly, we parted unreconciled and went home on separate trains or buses. Our friends shook their heads in amazement. As we were so obviously unsuited to each other, why did we stay together?

Jan's grace and patience seemed inexhaustible. Any other girl would have walked out on me long ago. I knew she stayed with me to help me. Perhaps she felt she must, for no one else would. But then something happened that stretched even Jan's resources to the limit.

One day at the office I found a hypodermic needle in a sink that only I normally used. A few days later I found another, then another. I reported it to the office manager and disclaimed any idea of how they had got there.

There was only one other ex-addict working at the office.

I challenged him about it, but he denied all knowledge of it. I believed him. I knew he was really going on with the Lord and had been off drugs longer than I had. But I couldn't explain it. It seemed unlikely, but I could only assume some drug addict was coming in from the street, using the public toilet in the building, and attempting to dispose of his used needles down my sink.

It was an embarrassing situation – and distressing for me. At first everyone in the office took my word that it was nothing to do with me. Then, more were found in my sink, and people began to look askance at me. Was I a liar? Had I gone back on drugs while pretending I had not?

No. I protested to the now disbelieving enquiries – I really didn't know anything about it – it was absolutely nothing to do with me!

One day, John took me aside and showed me a large envelope full of hypodermic needles and broken ampoules! The evidence against me, he said, seemed conclusive. It was very unlikely that a drug addict could walk in off the streets regularly and use my sink without being seen even once. It was also highly unlikely that the other ex-addict in the office was the culprit – even I had to admit that. The only other possible explanation was me!

I firmly protested my innocence and John left it at that. But I began to have doubts; it really couldn't be anyone else but me. Could I have done it without consciously knowing it? It seemed unlikely, but possible. It began to worry me. Then I had to face the suspicious glances of the other office workers every day. By now everyone seemed to believe I was living a lie, and the tension between us soon became unbearable.

One day after work I decided to go down to Piccadilly and buy a 'fix'. Everyone thought I was doing it already, so why not? If I was getting the blame, I reasoned, I may as well have the pleasure.

I spent several hours at Piccadilly, bought methodrine, and heroin, locked myself in a toilet, and shot the 'fix' into a vein. Suddenly, I didn't care what anyone thought. The 'fix' was nice. It was just like old times. Why bother trying to be a Christian? When the chips were down Christians were just the same as the rest – suspicious and condemning.

Then I thought of Jan – and wept. I felt sorry for myself – and sorry for Jan. At least, I told myself, she deserved an explanation. Still 'high' I found a telephone kiosk and rang her. Tearfully, I tried to explain what I had done and why – then I asked her not to tell John.

Later I went home to John's and Dawn's. As soon as I walked in the door I knew that Jan had telephoned John and told him. So, I thought, even Jan had let me down. When everyone had left the room, John asked me what it was all about. I told him everything, then broke down and wept. We prayed together, then I went to bed.

At breakfast next morning everything was normal. My lapse the day before had been forgiven by my Father and therefore forgotten by my family. I never shot another fix. It did transpire later that the syringes and needles were put in the sink by someone else. Everything was resolved.

When everyone else had left after breakfast and Dawn was in the kitchen, John came over and sat beside me.

'Don't you have a couple of weeks' holiday owing?' he asked.

'Yeah,' I said. 'Why?'

John patted my shoulder. 'I think you need a holiday,' he said.

'Any particular place in mind?' I asked him.

'Sidmouth,' John said. 'South Devon. I've got a friend, an ex-addict, down there. His name is Tony Ralls. It might do you good to spend a few days with him!'

'Okay,' I agreed.

The following week I took a train to Sidmouth. John was right. It was good to be away from London for a while. Fortunately the weather was good; it was hot and I was able to relax on the beach or swim in the sea.

Tony Ralls got me involved in everything he was doing in Sidmouth. He ran a coffee-bar for young people near the beach, and it seemed, these charismatic young people were having a tremendous effect in the local church.

'Two things I believe,' Tony said. 'If you've got anything

from the Lord it must be shared with others. I don't believe in holy huddles. And the other is that you have *everything* as a Christian potentially, but you must also make what you have *real* in experience.' We were walking along the beach.

'How do you mean exactly?' I asked.

'Well . . .' Tony said, 'take the sea for example. Now we know the tremendous potential for destruction it has. It could wipe out this entire town, and every other coastal town in one day. But look at it now. It is calm and beautiful. It is using its power to nibble away the land bit by bit.' Tony threw a pebble into the sea.

'That's like the Christian life,' he went on. 'All of us have exactly the same power at our disposal as each other – the same power that Christ talked about when He said, "Truly, truly, I say to you, he who believes in me will also do the works that I do, and greater works than these will he do, because I go to the Father. Whatever you ask in my name, I will do it, that the Father may be glorified in the Son; if you ask anything in my name I will do it." Many people live calm and beautiful Christian lives, but they are using this tremendous power only to nibble away at their problems. They never realise their full potential as Christians because they fail to turn that potential into real experience.'

'So how is it done?' I asked. Tony looked directly at me.

'From what you've told me,' he said, 'you already know. What you received that Easter Sunday, forgiveness, the Spirit of God, new birth, became a real *experience* when you were baptised in water, right?'

I nodded.

'And it happened because you were spiritually thirsty, desperately in fact?'

'That's right,' I said, 'I wanted to die rather than stay as I was.'

'Right,' Tony said. 'You experienced the fact of forgiveness of sin and new birth. What you need now is to experience the *power* of what you received at conversion.'

'How do I do that?' I asked. We sat on a rock near the water's edge. Tony pointed at the sea.

'What would it take to turn all that into a tremendously

destructive power?' he asked.

'Wind,' I said. Tony nodded.

'And all it takes to turn you or me, or any other Christian, into a tremendous power for good is wind. The wind of the Spirit.'

Tony opened his little New Testament, and read, 'But you shall receive power when the Holy Spirit has come upon you, and you shall be my witnesses in Jerusalem and in all Judaea and Samaria and to the end of the earth.'

'But the Holy Spirit has already come upon me,' I pointed out, 'when I was converted.'

'That's right,' Tony agreed. 'And the wind that could turn the sea into a tremendous power is already here.' Tony waved his hand in the air. 'But nothing is happening. It's exactly the same with the Holy Spirit in you now. It needs to be stirred up.'

'Are you talking about being baptised in the Spirit?' I asked. Tony nodded. Being a member of a Pentecostal church, I had heard about this. Many Christians in my church claimed to be 'baptised in the Spirit' but I wasn't impressed. This 'power for service' they all talked about seemed to be limited to shouting 'Hallelujah' or 'Praise the Lord' and clapping their hands in church – and speaking in tongues.

'So what will being baptised in the Spirit do for me?' I asked, waiting to pounce if he mentioned tongues.

'I don't know,' Tony said.

'What?' I asked in amazement. 'How do you mean you don't know?'

'The wind blows where it will,' Tony quoted. 'And you hear the sound of it, but you do not know where it comes or whither it goes – so it is with every one who is born of the Spirit.'

'All right,' I said. 'What do I do?'

'Nothing,' Tony said.

'Nothing?' I repeated.

'That's right,' Tony said. 'The Baptism in the Spirit is an Act of God, not man. All you can do is ask for it.'

I was getting annoyed. Obviously Tony wasn't going

out of his way to make it easy for me.

'And you won't ask until you are really thirsty,' he said, and then quoted another Scripture: 'If any one thirst, let him come to me and drink. He who believes in me, as the Scripture has said, "out of his heart shall flow rivers of living water". Now this he said about the Spirit, which those who believed in him were to receive; for as yet the Spirit had not been given, because Jesus was not yet glorified.'

'The point is' Tony continued, 'as a Christian you now have everything in Christ Jesus, forgiveness of sins, new birth, the Holy Spirit, and a secure inheritance – and many Christians never get any further than this – but you need to make it real in your *experience*.'

A few days later I went for a walk along the cliff-top to have a serious talk, alone, with God. I was confused. I knew I needed something but I didn't want to use another man's opinions or beliefs as a crutch to prop up my own flagging Christian life. I didn't understand all this talk about 'potential' and 'experience' – it sounded too much like hair-splitting to me. And besides, I hadn't noticed any significant difference between those who claimed to be baptised in the Spirit and me.

I found a quiet spot on the cliff-top. It was a grassy slope that ended in a sheer drop of several hundred feet. I sat down only two or three feet from the edge and started to talk to my Father. It was a beautiful clear day. I could see way across the ocean, and the people on the beach far below.

I asked God to show me what was wrong in my life, and how to put it right.

Suddenly, I felt myself starting to move. I was slipping down the slope towards the cliff-edge. I tried to dig in my heels and take hold of the grass. But the grass was slippery and I slid further and faster. My feet went over the edge and I saw myself falling through empty space to my death on the beach several hundred feet below.

'Lord,' I cried. 'Save me.'

The thought flashed through my mind that I was not yet

ready to die – not in a spiritually fit state to meet my God – and, suddenly, I realised how far short of His plan for my spiritual life I had fallen. I was aware of my need.

Then, I stopped. My legs were hanging over the precipice, but I had stopped moving. I sat trembling from head to foot, rooted with fear, but thanking and praising God. This was a real miracle of physical deliverance. I quoted God's words, 'For he will give his angels charge of you to guard you in all your ways. On their hands they will bear you up, lest you dash your foot against a stone.'

Then, I heard the voice of the Lord in my heart speak the rest of that passage of Scripture, 'You will tread on the lion and the adder, the young lion and the serpent you will trample under foot. Because he cleaves to me in love, I will deliver him; I will protect him, because he knows my name. When he calls to me, I will answer him: I will be with him in trouble. I will rescue him and honour him. With long life I will satisfy him, and show him my salvation.'

'Thank you, Lord,' I said. 'What do you want me to do?'

Then the Lord spoke to me again. 'Tonight I will baptise you in the Holy Spirit and I will manifest myself to you. You will be my witness and I will give you power over all the works of the evil one. You are my child, and I will be with you wherever I send you.'

Slowly, I turned and inched my way back up the slope. When I finally stood up, my legs felt like water, but I had a wonderful sense of the peace and presence of God in my heart.

That night Tony decided to have a praise and worship meeting for his young people – with special emphasis on the baptism of the Holy Spirit. Afterwards, Tony asked all those who recognised their need for this experience to go into another room.

Tony and several helpers prayed and laid hands on each one in turn. Almost all of them immediately spoke in tongues, shouting 'Hallelujah' and praising the Lord.

When Tony laid his hands on my head and prayed that I would be baptised in the Holy Spirit, strange words started coming out of my mouth too! I felt as if I had been lifted bodily off the floor, and I praised the Lord, and shouted 'Hallelujah', as enthusiastically as all the others. Suddenly, I felt a release of tension I hadn't been even aware of before, and the love of Jesus filling me as water fills an empty tank. I felt wonderfully calm inside and at peace with the whole world. I no longer wanted to attack everyone else, or defend myself, but was instead filled with love for them and an awareness of my own weakness.

When I returned to London I didn't need to explain what had happened to me. John and Dawn noticed the difference – and so did Jan.

Chapter Nine

A Night Visit

Suddenly, the Christian life was exciting. Until my visit to Sidmouth my Christian life had been a seesaw of 'highs' and 'lows'. I had never taken the time to look at it objectively.

Now, I did. And I could see how my Father had been using many people and many things to bring me to a real and deep awareness of my need.

Before Jesus had baptised me with the Holy Spirit I had been so taken up with *my* problems, *my* needs and *my* anxieties, the 'I' in me had been like a stopper in a bottle of fizz trying to 'pop'.

Being baptised with the Holy Spirit was for me the 'pop' – a release of the inner tension that had so often erupted in anger against others and in rebellion against God. Now I had a real assurance of salvation and a deep conviction that whatever happened the Father was with me.

Baptism with the Holy Spirit opened up my spirit in a new way. Although I was grateful for advice from other Christians I no longer needed to lean on them as I had previously.

My Father spoke to me *personally*, both in my spirit and through His word. That was another revelation – access to the throne of grace. One day, while I was praying and reading, the Lord directed my attention to the last few verses in Mark's Gospel: 'And He said to them, "Go into all the world and preach the gospel to all creation . . . And these signs will accompany those who believe: in my name they will cast out demons, they will speak with new tongues, they will pick up serpents, and if they drink any deadly poison, it shall not hurt them; they will lay hands on the sick, and they will recover." '

Although I had seen these same verses many times before, now they seemed to leap out at me. Suddenly I saw the weakness of Christ's church on earth – the same weakness that had almost turned me away from it. We were no longer doing what Jesus had commanded us to do – 'preach the gospel *and* heal the sick'.

As I prayed and re-read these verses, I knew I could not relegate them to the first century, and that if the Word of God was true then these verses must be relevant today.

I had spoken in tongues. But the word of God also declared: 'they will lay hands on the sick [Who? They who believed.] and they will recover [Why? As a confirmation of the gospel Jesus commanded us to preach]'.

Why hadn't I seen that before? Miracles of healings were not confined to specially gifted Christians but were an integral part of the proclamation of the gospel. Suddenly, Jesus spoke to my heart: 'This is why I have baptised you with the Holy Spirit to go and preach the gospel to all the world. You will tread on the lion and the adder, the young lion and the serpent you will trample underfoot.'

I was almost breathless with excitement. The Father had not only made me His son, He had also given me the power to beard the roaring lion and crush the snake who had kept me bound for so long – and I couldn't wait to get started.

Soon after my return from Sidmouth, I moved into a flat of my own in Fulham. Although I didn't ask her outright, I started dropping hints to Jan about marriage. But she managed to side-step them all. Now I was even more sure about the eventual outcome of our relationship, but I still had to convince Jan. Getting my own flat was part of it. I wanted Jan to see I could manage on my own and without depending on John and Dawn – independently dependent on God, as John called it.

Then I applied for admission to Bible College. I hadn't forgotten that part of God's plan for my life . . . and I wanted Jan to see I was thinking about the future.

Unfortunately I wasn't as good at housekeeping as I thought I might be. I couldn't cook for one thing, so I lived mainly on fish and chips and hamburgers. And I forgot to dust so that, eventually, clouds of dust rose in the air when I sat in an armchair or trod too hard on the carpet.

Occasionally Jan came over to cook me a 'proper meal' and clean up the flat. She brought me things to put in the refrigerator that only needed heating and made me promise to use them instead of fish and chips. But invariably I forgot, and when Jan came again the things she had brought last time were still in the fridge and going mouldy!

At least, I thought, she could see how much I needed her.

Now and then we spent an evening reading and praying, or listening to music. Often we went over to John and Dawn for fellowship – or a free meal. On special occasions – birthdays, or when the Lord sent us extra money – we went to the Royal Festival Hall. But usually we just walked along the Embankment.

A few months after moving to Fulham I woke up one night and heard someone knocking on my door. It was midnight and I had been sound asleep. Pulling on my dressing-gown I staggered sleepily down the stairs and opened the door. It was Jan – and she looked close to tears.

'What is it? Come in.' I said. 'What's wrong?'

'Nothing's wrong . . .' Jan said hesitantly. 'I just want to talk to you for a minute.' I closed the door and we went upstairs to my flat. I hoped none of the other tenants saw me walking up the stairs in my pyjamas with a girl. We sat on the settee and Jan looked at me.

'I love you,' she said. 'I just had to come and tell you.'

I sat and looked at her for a minute. We were more alike than either of us had thought. Coming to tell me she loved me at midnight was the kind of crazy thing I might have done. But calm and level-headed Jan? And me in my pyjamas too!

'That's marvellous,' I said. 'And I love you – you crazy thing.'

I dressed and walked Jan to the station. God's word to me seemed to be nearing fulfilment. At least as I told myself on the way back from the station, Jan was thinking along the right lines.

However, not all our friends were of the same mind. Most of them still thought Jan and I were unsuited, and this made Jan uncertain and fearful about our future together. We discussed it, but Jan could not come to a final decision. The Lord had given us many words of wisdom and comfort during our relationship, but for a life-long commitment to each other in marriage we both agreed that we needed something very definite, and for ever indisputable, from Him.

It wasn't very long in coming.

One Sunday afternoon we went to a meeting conducted by Jean Darnell. We had never been to any of her meetings before and knew very little about her. Jan and I sat in the middle of a row at the back of the crowded hall. I was sitting between Jan and another girl. There was nothing to indicate that Jan and I were together, as I spoke to the other girl as much as I did to Jan.

We sang several choruses, then listened to Jean Darnell preach. It was a good message and I could see that Jan was enjoying it too.

After the message Jean asked everyone to bow their heads while she prayed. As she prayed I looked up. Suddenly, Jean stopped praying, opened her eyes and looked straight at me. Then she pointed at me and said,

'You are with the girl on your right. You are a couple very much together. Is that right?' I was too surprised to answer, so I simply pointed at myself, silently enquiring whether she was really speaking to me.

'Yes,' Jean said, 'you in the brown tie.' I nudged Jan who was still praying with her head bowed. Jan looked up, and Jean addressed her.

'There is a great deal of uncertainty and fear in your heart about this relationship,' she said, 'but it will go. You must go ahead and take the step you are considering. For this is the will of God for you.'

Then Jean walked over to us and smiled at me.

'I think you have a remarkable testimony for us, don't you?'

'No . . .' I said in embarrassment. 'If you don't mind, I'd rather not.'

I had the feeling that God had revealed many things about us to Jean. And she had never seen us before. Another miracle. And, this time, Jan was part of it.

After the meeting Jean spoke to us again. I told her I had been on drugs but that God had delivered me from them and saved me – and I was cautious about giving my testimony.

Jean nodded understandingly and said she had felt it was something like that.

Then the Lord gave her another word of knowledge about us.

She said that all our friends were dubious about our marriage – but God was for it, and if what she had said was a confirmation of what God had spoken to our hearts in accordance with His written Word then we should go ahead and do it.

Soon, we were making plans for our wedding. Not long after that I received a letter accepting me into Bible College.

God had fulfilled both His promises.

The twentieth of August 1975, a date that I had waited for more impatiently than any other in my life, finally arrived. John Harris was our best man, and when Jan, a vision in white, came down the aisle to Dvorak's 'New World' symphony, I could hardly believe it was actually happening.

Somehow it all seemed so unreal. Afterwards, at the dinner, I told the guests, 'I'm not sure if I am in your dream, or you are in mine. But I feel as if any moment my alarm clock is going to ring and I am going to wake up and discover that this hasn't really happened.'

But it had. Another miracle that only God could have

brought about. We spent several days in beautiful Pitlochry, Perthshire, then it was back to England, and Bible College.

Now I was looking forward to studying His word in order to learn how to use the power God had promised to manifest through me.

Chapter Ten

Rebel

The harsh reality of Bible College was a sobering shock – not at all like my imaginative idea. In dreams I had seen myself dressed in white robes with a huge Bible under my arm walking up long marble stairs to golden doors with a big neon sign flashing 'Bible College'. Awake, I imagined it to be an idyllic period of feasting on the Word of God, of lightning-fast spiritual growth, and daily miracles all along the way.

The reality was like a slap in the face. We lived in a tiny attic room ten miles away from the Bible College. When Jan saw where we were going to spend the next three years of our lives – and possibly bring up children – she burst into tears.

'We can't live here,' she sobbed. 'There isn't enough room for a cat, never mind a baby . . .' I tried to joke about it but she was right. The tiny attic room looked awful. It had a bare wooden table, two wooden chairs, and an old very uncomfortable bed-settee – with a sink in one corner.

Jan started crying at two o'clock that day and didn't stop until she cried herself to sleep about midnight. I tried to comfort her as much as I could – but I was almost on the verge of tears too. The reality did not match the dream, and I couldn't explain it.

Until then both of us had experienced God's abundance

– even 'running over' – in providing for our material needs. We took the Word of God literally, asked our Father for what we needed, believed He would provide it and received it with joy and thanksgiving.

This was the first time we had received less than we had expected.

It was a long time before we realised – too late – that we had not asked specifically for *anything* regarding accommodation. We had been so excited about Bible College – and taken accommodation for granted – we had not really made it a matter of specific prayer. Now, it looked as if we were in this tiny attic for the duration.

While we were waiting for my grant to be approved – which *had* been a matter of specific and urgent prayer – Jan decided to take a job. We calculated that we needed seventeen pounds a week to live, so we prayed that whatever job Jan got her wages would be that amount.

Jan finally got a part-time job as a 'tea lady' in a local insurance office, and her first week's wages after stoppages were seventeen pounds and four pence. We decided the extra four pence was for Jan to write home, which we hadn't included in our original calculations!

When my grant was approved six weeks later we discovered it was the highest grant in the entire college. It was so much I was the only student on a grant who didn't need to work during the holidays. I was able to spend more time with Jan – and make up for some of the time lost at the college.

The first year went smoothly. Much to my surprise, I found studying easy. I had a gift for reading a text book in a few hours and assimilating all the material so that I could pass an exam with credit on that subject the next year. I did so well – particularly in Greek – in my first year I decided to study for a degree in my second year.

At the beginning of my second year Jan gave birth to a beautiful little girl. We named her Laura Elizabeth – but trouble started from the day we brought her home from the hospital.

She cried almost continuously. For the next eighteen

months little Laura didn't sleep one night through. We took alternate nights sitting up with her. When it was my turn, the next day I found myself nodding off during lectures. Finally, I had to abandon all hope of gaining a degree and decided I would be fortunate if I passed even the basic college course.

During those three years the Lord taught Jan and me a great deal about ourselves, other people, and Him. It was a time of the file, the hammer and the fire. We were drawn even closer together in our tiny attic room, made more outgoing by the college outreach in our cities and towns, and more independently dependent on the Lord for our daily needs.

From the start of my Bible College training I was a rebel. It wasn't done wilfully. If anything I would rather have gone unnoticed. I simply wanted to learn as much as possible as quickly as I could by asking questions rather than simply filling exercise-books with reams of notes. I seemed to have a mental block when it came to notes, and rebelled against the notion of transferring the lecturer's notes into my notes and bypassing my brain. No one else seemed to worry about it. Most of the other students were newly out of school and were used to this method.

Some of the questions I asked embarrassed even the lecturers.

'But what is the unforgivable sin?' I enquired of one.

The poor man stuttered and sweated as he tried to summarise everything he had ever read about it, the argument of early theologians and modern opinion.

'But what does the Bible say about it?' I insisted. Apparently the Bible, or so he declared, wasn't very clear on the precise nature of the 'unforgivable sin'.

I refused to accept that and, during the next break between lectures, I searched the Scriptures for myself. When the bell went for the next lecture, with the same lecturer, I was armed and ready.

I stood up, opened my Bible at Mark's Gospel, and announced: 'Sir, I have the answer to the question I asked in the last period.'

The lecturer smiled weakly at me and tried to put me off by waving me back in my seat. I refused to be cut off, and remained standing.

'Sir . . .' I repeated, 'I do have the answer.'

'Very well,' he said with a trace of annoyance. 'What is it you want to say?'

I read from chapter three, beginning at verse twenty-eight.

'Truly, I say to you, all sins will be forgiven the sons of men, and whatever blasphemies they utter; but whoever blasphemes against the Holy Spirit never has forgiveness, but is guilty of an eternal sin.'

The rest of the class looked at me in silence, then looked at the lecturer. He coughed nervously, then announced to the class: 'Very well, you may add that to your notes.'

Later that day I was called into the office used by the director of studies. He was a kindly man, and understood my difficulty in merely copying down notes.

'As a student . . .' he paused for thought. 'It's your duty to listen, not argue.'

'But I wasn't arguing,' I protested. 'I just want to know the truth.'

The director of studies smiled.

'Well, I very much hope we do teach the truth, but I would rather you think it out for yourself, receive what you can, and leave the rest. After all, we can't have two lecturers in one class can we?'

I promised to restrain myself in the future. But even as I said it I knew I wouldn't be able to do it for very long.

Another lecturer spent almost an entire period extolling Sigmund Freud. I stayed seated for as long as I could, then suddenly I lost control when the lecturer declared, 'Sigmund Freud has done more for me than anyone else.'

'Well,' I leapt to my feet. 'Jesus has done more for me, and for every other born-again believer, than anyone.' The lecturer was very angry.

'Such a statement reveals how very simple minded you are!' she declared. 'Of course Jesus has done a great deal more for us than any man, but when you are speaking to men of the world you must learn how to relate to them. What I might say in church is not what I would say in the market-place. You can't say in the market-place what you can say in church.'

'Rubbish! If you can't say it in church, you shouldn't be saying it at all. And if what you say in the market-place doesn't tie up with what you say in church, you are a hypocrite!'

Admittedly, I had gone much too far that time. The lady lecturer went scarlet with embarrassment and rage, picked up her notes and walked out.

This time it was the principal's office. The principal shuffled the pages of my college report as he listened to my explanation for my behaviour in class. 'I'm not even sure that woman is born again,' I concluded.

The principal looked at me over his spectacles.

'I've known Mrs. Johnson since she was a little girl,' he said, 'and I can assure you, she most certainly is.' We sat in silence for a few moments.

'John, I'm not at all sure that you are settling down at this college very well,' the principal said ominously. 'We have all done our best to understand your special problems, and to help you as much as we possibly could. I should be extremely distressed if we had to ask you to leave . . .'

I said nothing. The principal cleared his throat, then went on, 'But if there are any other similar incidents, I'm very much afraid we shall have to. Do you understand?'

I said I did and promised, again, to control myself better.

Jan was my anchor. Many times I wanted to give up and walk out of college.

'I can't go on,' I moaned at her. 'I'm just no good. Everybody thinks differently from me. I might as well give up.'

'Give up?' she exclaimed. 'Give up on God, give up on me.' Jan put her arms round me. 'I want my husband to do great things for God, but before He will use you He has to deal with all that pride in you.'

Jan was right, as usual. Because I was much older than the other students, and had more experience of life, I reacted against what I saw as a willingness to soak up anything without question.

'It's better to be right than wrong,' Jan said, 'but sometimes it's more loving to be wrong.'

That was a lesson in humility. And it was put to the test before my graduation.

Just before the final exam marks were published, there was an uproar among the students. Apparently some of the lecturers had the habit of noting down our examination marks on odd scraps of paper, old envelopes, or even on the back of their hands, until they had time to put them on file.

As a result, some marks had never reached the file and were lost. In the last-minute panic to find out which marks had been lost, old essays were called in. However, by that time most of us had lost them or thrown them away.

Usually I destroyed mine as soon as they had been marked. Now, the director of studies informed me that unless I could find them my marks would have to be reduced from honours to credit as he had only half my marks on file.

I was furious.

'I won't accept it,' I stormed at Jan. 'I'll stand on that graduation platform and refuse it. I'll tell the whole world about the mess they've made!'

'And bring the college into disrepute?' Jan asked. 'For what, to tell everybody how brilliant you are? No. What does it matter what the world thinks? God knows!'

It was the hardest thing in my life to stand on that platform on graduation day and receive my certificate of credit, instead of honours, but it was a lesson well learned.

Chapter Eleven

Whatsoever You Ask

Another lesson was even more traumatic. It happened during my last few weeks at college.

The time for us to move out of our student accommodation was fast approaching, but we had nowhere else to go. Admittedly, I had left it rather late. Jan became increasingly anxious, and tearful, as time went by without any positive sign of where we were to live.

The day we married, Jan and I made a vow to each other before the Lord that so long as we owned to the Father as our provider we would never accept financial credit, or deliberately go into debt. There were times when we went down to our last penny – literally – but, each time, He supplied all we needed, and often much more than we asked.

This time, however, nothing seemed to be happening. One door after another was closed against us. We had very little money, certainly not enough even for a deposit on a caravan, and the waiting-list for council houses everywhere we enquired were years long.

Although the college didn't want to throw us out on the street, new students had to be accommodated, and they needed every room. Time was fast running out. I went out each day, only to come back even more dejected.

Finally, in absolute desperation, and at the eleventh hour – only three days before we had to leave – I decided to hand over the problem completely to the Lord. I took my Bible and told Jan I was going to the park to read and pray and would not come back until the Lord had given me a clear and very definite word about this situation. Jan knew I meant it and promised to support me by doing the same.

In the park I lay on the grass with my Bible open and started talking to my Father. There were people constantly walking by, and two ladies came and sat on a bench not far away from me. But it was far too late to worry about what people might think.

First, I confessed my lack of total dependence on God in not bringing this problem to Him sooner, and asked forgiveness. Then I boldly reminded the Lord that He had given a promise in His Word that suited our situation perfectly: 'Truly, I say to you, there is no one who has left house or brothers or sisters or mother or father or children or lands, for my sake and for the gospel, who will not receive a hundredfold now in this time, houses and brothers and sisters and mothers and children and lands, with persecutions, and in the age to come eternal life.'

Well, I reminded the Lord, we had done that. We had left our employment, our home, and everything that might have been ours to go to Bible College in obedience to Him. Now, I insisted, we were His responsibility.

If the last part of that verse about eternal life was true, I reasoned, then so was the first part about a hundred houses. I didn't mind the persecutions so much, I went on, but I intended to hold Him to the 'now in this time' promise as well.

I talked to my Father for over an hour, reading passages from His Word in between, when suddenly, He gave me the word I was seeking. 'I know your works . . . Behold, I have set before you an open door, which no one is able to shut; I know that you have but little power, and yet you have kept my word and have not denied my name.'

Satisfied, and filled with a deep assurance, I went home. Jan greeted me with a big smile and told me that the Lord had given her a verse of Scripture. She read, ' "Behold, I have set before you an open door . . ." An open door,' she said excitedly. 'That means a house, doesn't it?'

'Well . . .' I laughed. 'If we take the Word of God literally, it means a hundred houses.'

The very next day someone telephoned me and advised me where to go and whom to see about a house. It was the Development Corporation in Peterborough. Before we went we decided that if the Lord was going to give us a house then it might as well be exactly the kind of house we really wanted. So we spent a few days telling the Lord how many rooms we wanted, the size of the garden, and the colour and particular style of décor we liked.

When we went to Peterborough we were shown a list of *several hundred* houses. So far, it seemed, the Lord was *literally* performing his Word. But how to choose? When I was told that Christians had previously lived in one particular house the Lord said to me, 'That's the one, take it.' And so it was. The house had even been recently decorated in exactly the colour Jan wanted!

The next thing we had to do was find the money to move the things we had collected from Dorking to Peterborough. We discovered it would cost two hundred pounds and we didn't have two hundred pence, but knowing the Lord always completes what He begins we got down to some very serious praying.

It was our policy not to mention any need we were currently praying about to anyone, and to pray for only the exact amount we needed. We wanted to make sure that we didn't confuse effective prayer with the kindness of friends.

Two days later an envelope dropped through our letter-box. Inside was two one hundred pound notes! The money had been sent by someone who had not heard from us for years and didn't know anything about our present financial problem.

When we finally said our farewell to our friends in Dorking, Jan and I knew we had gained far more than a merely academic knowledge of the Word of God. So many times we had put it to the test of our need, and each time it had proved true.

One of the conditions attached to possession of our new home was that I had to be in full-time employment from the first Monday after moving in, otherwise the agreement would be void and we would lose the house. But, as the Lord had also provided me with a job on a local building site through another Christian in the town, this was no problem and we spent that first weekend organising the house and praising the Lord.

On Monday, however, I was coming down the stairs when my back gave way. I lay on the living-room floor in great pain and unable to move. I'd had trouble with my back since the age of eight when I had leapt off a high roof on to a concrete path. I had been to the doctors and osteopaths and found temporary relief, but it had never been cured. Now it happened again. I couldn't even stand up let alone go to work on a building site – and we were in trouble.

'What are we going to do?' I groaned helplessly. Jan looked worried, then had an idea.

'Do you remember when Peter and John saw the lame man lying at the Beautiful Gate?' she asked.

'Yes,' I said, wondering what this had to do with our present predicament.

'Well,' she went on, 'didn't they just *command* the man to get up and walk in the name of Jesus?'

'That's right. They certainly did!'

'Well, I believe this is an attack of Satan,' Jan said. 'So this is a good time to see if we really do have power over the work of the Evil One. Let's just command this infirmity to go, in the name of Jesus.'

'Okay,' I agreed. 'Go ahead.'

Jan kneeled beside me and laid her hands on my back. 'In the name of Jesus . . .' she commanded, 'I rebuke this work of Satan and command this infirmity to go – and never come back.'

Immediately the pain vanished and I was able to stand up. Carefully, I touched my toes once or twice, then twisted my body round.

'Praise the Lord,' we both shouted in unison, and hugged each other. Before I went off to work we prayed and re-read Jesus's promise to His followers in Mark's Gospel: 'And these signs will accompany those who believe: in my name they will cast out demons, they will speak in new tongues; they will pick up serpents, and if they drink any deadly thing, it will not hurt them; they will lay their hands on the sick, and they will recover.'

That day I carried huge loads of slates up ladders without so much as a twinge. And my back trouble has never recurred since!

We hadn't been in our new home very long when the Lord revealed to Jan and me the *extent* of His power available to us through prayer.

The Lord had filled our home with furniture – and one of the most welcome gifts for Jan was a new and very expensive automatic washing machine. While we had been at Dorking Jan had washed everything by hand in a tiny sink. But, for a brand-new house, we felt a washing machine was needed. So we prayed and the Lord provided.

One day, for no apparent reason, it wouldn't start. Jan and I pushed every available button and turned the dials, but the machine remained totally lifeless. Ordinarily, I would have checked the plug and then, if necessary, telephoned the repair man as the machine was new and under guarantee. This time I decided to try something else. 'How about praying that the Lord will make it work?' I asked Jan. She didn't look so sure.

'*Anything you ask* . . .' I reminded her. '*Nothing* shall be impossible to you . . .'

So far we had prayed for material provision and physical healing and had seen those prayers answered, but we had never prayed for an inaminate object – for a miracle pure and simple – and I was eager to try.

'All right,' Jan said, 'go ahead.'

A little apprehensively I laid my hand on the machine and said simply, 'In the name of Jesus – work.'

Then Jan pushed the start button again – and the machine immediately whirred into action! We looked at each other then laughed with joy.

'We're in the Lord's Bible College now,' I said. 'And the graduation prize isn't a diploma. It's the crown of life eternal.'

Chapter Twelve

Stumbling Lips

People often ask me, 'How is it you seem to find living a victorious Christian life so easy, while I, with a good Christian upbringing, find it all an uphill struggle? It seems so unfair.'

Well, the simple truth is that *I* don't. I have failed in many ways, been cast down, fearful, and at the point of despair. In one sense, the Christian life isn't easy. But it should always be exciting, a glorious adventure and an inspiring challenge.

When I first gave my heart and life to Christ, I thought I should be doing well if my Christian life lasted six months. Nothing I had tried before had ever lasted that long and, with all my good intentions, I knew it would take nothing less than a miracle to see me through even six months.

Part of that miracle was Jan. If Paul, like many others, needed a thorn to keep him humble, I needed a rose to keep me sweet!

Jan was God's instrument in forming and shaping my early Christian life. We often argued, but instead of trying to push she bent like a reed in order to lead my Christian experience in the right direction, then stood firm as an oak if I veered off.

One particular hang-up I had was the loss of my writing ability. I talked about it often, but never did anything about it. I criticised almost every book I read solely on the basis of bad style.

One day Jan showed me a children's story in a Christian magazine.

'Rubbish!' I said, after only a cursory glance.

'Well, why not write a better one?'

'I just might,' I said, 'one of these days.' Jan flopped in an armchair.

'Why not now?'

I gave her a withering look.

'You can't write stories just like that.'

Jan shook her head.

'No,' she agreed. 'I can't, but you can.'

'How do y'mean?'

'Write me a children's story, right now. I know you can do it.'

'No I can't. That disappeared years ago.'

Jan wouldn't be put off.

'Try. I'll help,' she urged me. 'I'll make it up, and you write it.'

Suddenly I started to sweat. I hadn't written anything in ten years. I had hoped that God would resurrect my writing ability after I had become a Christian, but it seemed He hadn't.

Jan had put me on a spot. Either I had to write something or stop criticising the writings of others, no matter how bad it was. I saw through Jan's scheme, so I agreed just to prove my point.

'Good.' Jan squealed with delight. 'This will be fun. I've never collaborated with a writer before!'

We started. Jan told the story, and I wrote. When I got stuck, or my interest waned, Jan cajoled until I wrote the next line.

For four hours, line by line, I wrote, then finally inscribed 'The End', and put down my pen. I was exhausted, but strangely excited, and waited anxiously while Jan read the story.

'It's great!' Jan grinned at me. 'It's a lovely story.'

I read it over for myself, then looked at Jan.

'Y'know . . .' I began, 'y'know this is the first story I've written in ten years.'

Jan nodded and touched my hand.

'What did I say?' she asked. 'I said you could do it. One day God will use your writing for His glory.'

I wasn't too sure about that, but it was a good story. It wasn't very much, but it was a beginning, and if I could do one . . .

Another hang-up was public speaking. Large crowds of people terrified me. I knew God had called me to preach, but each time I was asked to give my testimony I dried up.

One day I received an invitation to preach at the Westminster Central Hall in London. Jan was excited for me.

'But it's Westminster Central Hall!' I repeated. 'That's where all the big Evangelists preach.'

Jan laughed. 'But it's only a lunch-hour service,' she said. 'There probably won't be more than thirty people altogether. They won't eat you!'

'I can't,' I moaned. 'What if I dry up? The embarrassment . . .'

Jan shook her head. 'You won't,' she said confidently. 'You want to be a preacher, don't you? Well, there's no better place to start than the Westminster Central Hall! Forget about yourself. Let the Lord speak through you.'

That night I decided to write out what I was going to say the next day. I wrote, crossed out, rewrote – then started again. The night wore on. I was tired, but I pressed on. Suddenly, I noticed it was lighter. I opened the curtains and looked at my watch. It was eight-thirty. I had been writing since ten-thirty the previous night – and I still hadn't worked out what I was going to say.

I was in despair. Perhaps I could get out of it? Pretend I was sick – or simply not go? I thought about it. I didn't mind letting people down. But how could I explain it to Jan? What would *she* think of me?

As I washed and shaved I had an imaginary conversation with Jan. 'Well, love,' I sighed, 'it looks as if you're right, I'm going to have to trust the Lord.'

Jan telephoned me just before lunch to wish me well and said she would meet me after the service. 'I'll be praying for you,' she said. Me too, I thought as I put down the receiver. On the bus going to Westminster Central Hall I had a flash of inspiration and quickly jotted down six points I thought I would use for my sermon.

While the small congregation was singing the opening hymn I opened my Bible and looked at my brief notes.

'O Lord,' I pleaded silently. 'Help.' I couldn't even read what I had written, let alone remember what I had planned to say. The congregation sat down, and I stood up, trembling from head to toe.

I remembered a story that John Harris had told me about one of his first preaching experiences. He was so scared that, after the opening hymn, he asked everyone to bow their heads in prayer. While the congregation was praying John slipped out of a side door and went home.

'Well?' a voice whispered in my ear. 'Why shouldn't you? Go ahead.'

'Let's pray,' I announced. There was a door only a few feet away. I looked at the congregation. They all had their eyes closed. It would be easy to sneak out. As I was debating with myself about this, another voice said, 'Open your Bible at Mark chapter five. Now tell my people about the Gerasene demoniac. Tell them what it is to be in bondage, and tell them what it is to be delivered.'

I spoke for an hour. The congregation seemed to soak up every word. One lady stood up and ran out in tears. When I had finished there were more wet eyes, and many were murmuring 'Praise the Lord' and 'Wonderful Jesus' as they shook hands with me at the door.

'How did it go?' Jan asked a little anxiously.

'Great,' I said. 'How else?'

'You didn't dry up?'

'Dry up?' I asked. 'I didn't even start.' Then I told her the whole story.

'It was a strange feeling,' I concluded. 'I didn't think those people *saw* me at all. They were seeing Jesus.'

'Praise the Lord!' Jan laughed, then was serious. 'Don't

ever let them see anyone else. He is all you have.'

Jan was right. I was no theologian, or eloquent preacher. I was an ex-drug addict and all I had was Jesus. I promised myself that from then on He would be my only message, the Bible my only notes and the Holy Spirit my only inspiration.

Today, I believe that Jan and I have a marriage second to none. Strangers and friends who once thought our marriage would never work, think we now even look alike. We have been asked more than once if we are brother and sister! Recently we both completed a marriage quiz. Every answer was exactly the same. This, I believe, is evidence of how the Lord has fused us together.

At a time when many couples – thrown together by unemployment, the recession, and early retirement – are finding great difficulty in sharing time together, we cannot get enough. The more we are together, the closer we become, the more alike.

Coming from an unhappy home myself I used to worry that I lacked the experience of a loving well-adjusted home necessary to the building of another. Yet the transforming power of Jesus Christ has overflowed abundantly. What I lack He supplies. He is provider, counsellor, and head of our home. We rest safe and secure in His hand.

Next to my conversion, I see the relationship between Jan and me as the Lord's greatest miracle in my life. All the others, wonderful as they are, pale in comparison. Spectacular miracles of healing, deliverance and protection often take precedence in our minds over the daily miracles of nature. We take for granted the sustaining activity of God in nature, and forget that human relationships ordained by Him are also miracles of His grace.

The Lord has used Jan as His minister to me – without fanfare or public acclaim. In our relationship I have had all the publicity. As a converted drug addict I have been called a 'Trophy of Grace', and have been in demand as a speaker. Yet only God knows what might have become of me had it not been for Jan.

Chapter Thirteen

Run With The Wind

After the relatively easy pace of life at Bible College, life out in the big world seemed hectic. Being certain that God had called me to preach the gospel and heal the sick, I took advantage of every opportunity.

Jan and I joined the local Elim Pentecostal church in Peterborough, then a small fellowship of between fifteen and twenty people meeting in a Community Centre.

With my passion for evangelism it wasn't long before I was appointed director of evangelism, then I was accepted as a probationary minister with a brief to start an Elim church in an unevangelised area in Peterborough.

To me, preaching and healing the sick were inextricably bound together – two halves of the same gospel. I could not envisage preaching the gospel without healing the sick. In the Gospels Jesus always links the two together. In Acts, too, almost every miracle is either preceded or followed by the proclamation of the gospel.

I found that people more readily listened to the gospel, and received it, when its power was visibly demonstrated. Many gave their hearts and lives to the Lord on the street, on buses and in their own homes in response to the work of the Holy Spirit in physical healing.

A young girl caught by family heritage in Mormonism and who had been blinded in one eye in an accident as a child enthusiastically received Jesus as her personal Saviour standing at her door *after* the Lord instantly restored her sight.

A young man I met in a railway station was healed of a stomach cancer *after* he received Christ into his heart. A year later he wrote to me and said, 'I've just had another check up and the specialist says there is absolutely no trace of a cancer. Because of this miracle my dad has also given his heart to Jesus, and an aunt, an uncle and three neighbours. We all go to church together now.'

The Lord's grace and power have been demonstrated in many other ways. Once I travelled to Sheffield, my home town, to pray for a sick relative. After anointing the sick relative with oil and praying the prayer of faith, I witnessed to several unsaved people in the room who readily accepted Christ.

Later, another neighbour, who had been caring for the sick relative and had a remarkable reputation for good in the neighbourhood, came in. Apparently everyone loved her as a shining example of Christian character. She had been a regular church attender for more years than I had yet lived. I was so taken in by this lady's self-sacrifice and self-confessed diligence in prayer and Bible reading I asked her to join the rest of us in praying for my sick relative – to which she immediately and enthusiastically agreed.

However, just as I was about to pray, the Lord spoke to me in what seemed to be a very audible voice. 'This woman does not belong to me,' He said. 'She is an adultress. He is a coloured man, and his name is George. Rebuke this sin in her life, and I will breathe my Spirit upon her.'

I looked round the group, thinking everyone must have heard the words. Apparently no one had. I was horrified. Suppose I was wrong? What would she think of me? For an instant I hesitated. If no one else had heard the voice, wouldn't it be better if I forgot it and carried on with the prayer?

Suddenly, the Lord spoke to me again. He said, 'I have given you power to tread on the lion and the adder, the young lion and the serpent you will trample beneath your feet. Speak as I command you.'

Immediately, I asked the lady to go with me into an empty room where I could speak to her privately. I was still unsure. If this revelation was merely the invention of an over-active imagination, I was about to accuse a highly respected woman of adultery.

However, my reputation was not important and I would rather risk offending this woman than risk disobeying the Lord, so I spoke as He had directed. In the privacy of that room, the lady burst into tears of real repentance, confessed that I was right in every detail and received Jesus Christ as her personal Saviour.

Sometimes the Lord did something with the sick other than heal them. One such instance was Peggy Rainbow. Her daughter telephoned me and asked if I would visit her to discuss some evangelistic literature I had put through her door.

Over coffee that afternoon we discussed the need for a personal relationship with Jesus Christ. Before she had finished her coffee Jenny asked Jesus into her life and promised to follow Him from that moment on.

As I was making ready to leave, Jenny suddenly asked if I believed that Jesus still healed the physically ill today.

'Yes, indeed.' I smiled. 'Jesus is the same yesterday, today and for ever.'

Jenny then told me the real reason she had asked me to call. She wanted to ask me to pray for her mother, who was dying from cancer. Her mother, Peggy Rainbow, lived in Boston, a town about forty miles from Peterborough, with her husband, Maurice, and she had been ill many years.

I promised to visit Peggy as soon as possible, and the following week I did, finding her in bed and in great pain. Her skin was ash grey, she was terribly thin and extremely weak. Maurice arranged chairs round Peggy's bed for me, his two daughters and their husbands, and himself.

First, I explained the way of salvation as clearly and simply as I was able. Peggy responded immediately and gave her life to Christ. Then I anointed her with oil, laid my hands on her head and claimed her healing in His name.

The pain vanished immediately and completely and Peggy declared she felt better, in body and spirit, than she had for years.

The following week Maurice accepted Christ, and Peggy was able to get out of bed.

Over the next three weeks Maurice's two daughters, one of the husbands, and a visiting relative, all gave their lives to Christ – and Peggy continued to improve.

During this time the Rainbow family and I grew very close. I began to regard Peggy as my second mother. The Rainbows thought of me as an adopted son.

The next few months were wonderful. Peggy made good progress, and we made plans to share our joy and faith in the Lord with the rest of Boston. There were occasions when Peggy's condition seemed to deteriorate, but we held on to the promise of God.

Then, one day, Peggy suddenly died. I was stunned. How could God possibly let us down? We were all ready to begin witnessing in Boston – to share the good news that Jesus saves and still heals the sick today. But how could we declare that message now? And what about the other members of the Rainbow family, whose faith rested on the conviction that Jesus is the same yesterday, today and for ever.

I conducted Peggy's funeral with a heavy heart. Strangely, it was those I feared for most, the Rainbow family, who helped me during this dark period of doubt and near despair. Although he had lost his wife and life-long companion, Maurice did not lose his faith.

When I found the courage to ask how he really felt about Peggy's dying after all our praying and believing, he said, 'God has given us far more than we asked or even thought. Peggy is with Jesus. She isn't sick, or in pain. And all my family belongs to Him. God gave us much more than we asked or even thought.'

Later, Jenny wrote to me and said, 'through Mum's death, God brought us all together as a family. He has changed all our lives. Dad is a different man since Jesus came into his life. He is so happy. I am different, too, now that I have found Christ and His plan for my life. If Mum had lived, I think we would not have become Christians, but dying, God brought us all to see our need of Him . . .'

There is healing in death and through death, for Jesus is Lord of life and conqueror over death.

About this time, I felt it right to leave the Elim ministry. From then on, I ministered independently wherever and whenever I could.

The Lord's promise to be with me wherever He sent me often manifested itself in some dramatic ways. On one occasion I was on my way home from a Bible study. I had to go up a dark alley to get to the street where I lived.

Nothing unusual happened, and I arrived home still thinking about all I had learned of the Lord in the Bible study and rejoicing in Him. I was very much aware of His presence all the rest of the evening, and finally went to bed after a particularly blessed time of praise and worship.

Early the next morning there was a knock at my door. A big, unshaven coloured man stood there, his eyes staring at me and his mouth twitching uncontrollably. As he looked in need I invited him in. After a cup of coffee, he seemed to be calmer and told me his story. Apparently, the night before, he had seen me go into the alley on my way home and, in desperate need of money, thought I looked easy enough to beat up and rob. He followed me into the alley and was about to run up to me and hit me on the head with an iron bar when two strange figures suddenly appeared between him and me. They were shining, and seemed to be carrying cudgels or small swords. The coloured man stopped and watched. As I walked on, unaware of anything out of the ordinary, the two shining figures moved with me.

He followed the three of us to my door. When I went in the two figures stood outside the door, one on each side.

The coloured man watched for some time, then, shaking with fear, turned and ran away. He lay awake all that night in a cold sweat at what he had seen. He had come back this morning to ask my forgiveness, and to hear how I had 'acquired' my two guardians.

When I told him whom I supposed they might have been,

his eyes almost popped out of his head.

'Angels?' he repeated. 'Can I have two as well?' An hour later the coloured man, Henry, had given his heart and life to the Lord – and I assured him that now he had angels to guard him. He left that morning with food in his stomach, a little money in his pocket, a big smile on his face and, most important of all, with Jesus in his heart.

Chapter Fourteen

Abundant Living

About a year after leaving Bible College, Jan and I went through a particularly difficult financial period. Although the Lord was meeting our immediate needs in terms of basic necessities, we both felt that Scripture promised much more for believers than the minimum standard of living.

We made this a matter of long discussion and special prayer. Personally, I have never believed that 'living by faith' – meaning looking to the Lord entirely for financial provision – is incumbent on *every* Christian.

Immediately after Bible College I worked as a labourer on a building site, then as a clerk in an office. Although Jan and I had experienced the Lord's provision in many remarkable instances, and knew others who lived entirely 'by faith', we knew that, as yet, the Lord had not told us to do the same.

As a Christian and a minister of the gospel, I had long made a point of not seeming less affluent, in terms of my family's appearance, than our neighbours. If we were to witness to them successfully, we could not be thought of as impoverished, so bringing disrepute on the name of the Father whose children we claimed to be.

Then I saw that the same principle must apply to my children also. What was the point of preaching the 'abundant' supply of my heavenly Father if my own children lacked the things my non-Christian neighbours' children enjoyed? And how could I explain to them that my Father's provision did not extend to such things as games, dolls and toys?

The inner conviction that in fact it did extend so far eventually became so strong within my spirit I could not lay it aside. One day, just before Christmas, I knew that God had called Jan and me to live for Him entirely 'by faith'.

I don't think I could have chosen a worse time of the year to step out in this way. We had nothing in the bank, and the time for Christmas presents was fast approaching. Nor could I have chosen a worse year. There were over two million people unemployed, businesses were going into liquidation almost daily, and even the giant commercial enterprise I.C.I. was losing money for the first time in fifty years.

But God is master of the impossible! By Christmas our children had everything they had asked for – and more. From then on money poured in almost daily. While our neighbours were losing their jobs and having to cut back financially, our standard of living rose so dramatically we were able to give to our now impoverished neighbours, and witness to them in a clearly visible and practical way.

Jan and I had no idea where the money came from, and we never did find out. We had told no one about our needs or the step of faith. Money was pushed through the letter-box in an assortment of different envelopes – and at embarrassing moments.

Once I had testified about our manner of living to a group of Christians we did not know very well. I related how Jan and I had decided before the Lord never to borrow money or otherwise go into debt to man. Although I thought I had made it clear that this was a personal decision and not a general Scriptural rule for every believer, my testimony was received badly – and with more than a little scepticism! We later discovered that most of that group were in debt, and their minister had just taken out a large bank loan.

But the Lord is gracious. While we were having a

meeting at my home, a thick envelope was pushed through the letter-box. Knowing that it probably contained money, and the attitude of this group to my testimony, I thought it best to wait until everyone had gone home before opening it. But Jan insisted that I opened it there and then in front of the scoffers and doubters. I couldn't have invented a better visual aid! Inside was fifty pounds, just enough to provide for a specific need.

Soon after, the minister visited me and informed me that I was free to teach anything I liked – except the Lord providing money.

It was a lesson well learned. From then on I carefully observed the Biblical injunction: ' . . . the faith that you have, keep between yourself and God'. It is not well to talk about the delights of feasting to a starving man!

As a postscript to this story, the minister later cancelled his bank loan in faith, and afterwards received several hundred pounds from an unexpected source, and several of his congregation who had previously scorned my testimony dared to trust the Lord in various ways for finances and found Him faithful!

I am convinced that receiving from the Lord in this way can often be blocked by our lack of giving. The Lord did not prosper me as He does now before He taught me this principle of giving first.

It was at a large Pentecostal church in London. I had been particularly blessed by the service, and during the final hymn while the offering was being taken, I slipped my hand in my pocket and started hunting for coins.

Suddenly, I noticed that many others were doing exactly the same! I had several pound notes in my wallet and here I was searching for coins. Just then the Lord spoke to my heart. He said: 'John, this isn't the thing – it's tipping!' That truth hit home. I was offering the Lord no more than I would give a waitress or a taxi-driver.

I repented immediately, and as 'fruits of repentance' emptied the contents of my wallet into the offering plate – which meant I had nothing left except the loose change in my pocket, and my next pay was still a whole week away.

But I reckoned it a small price to pay for peace of mind and heart. However, the next morning at the office where I worked I found an envelope addressed to me. Inside was seven times the amount of money I had put into the offering the night before!

There was no note of explanation. No one in the office, so far as I knew, went to church, or had shown any interest in my own Sunday activity. But on the back of the envelope was the Christian sign of the fish.

From that time on I learned to tithe joyfully and give enthusiastically. The world says, 'Make as much as possible, save all you can, and give nothing away', but Jesus says '. . . give, and it will be given to you; good measure, pressed down, shaken together, running over, will be put into your lap' (Luke 6: 38).

Jan and I have found this to be true. Now, when we have a financial need, we give the little we have and the Lord returns His abundance!

Once, our faith stumbled. We had been receiving money through the letter-box for about six months. I knew that Jan was becoming increasingly nervous about where it was coming from. Was it stolen? Should we get into trouble if we spent it?

I tried to calm her anxiety and encouraged her to praise the Lord for His provision and not fear what man might do. But, suddenly, one morning Jan's fear turned into action.

'I'm sorry, Lord. But this scares me! Will you please stop it?'

That morning was the first time in six months we received no money. And, apart from an occasional gift from people we knew, the flow of money stopped.

Often in our Christian lives we have to learn old lessons afresh. This happened to Jan and me as, living on social security payments, we entered a period of 'spiritual calm'. It seemed nothing of significance was happening.

A book I was reading at the time told of a converted drunkard, and all the wonderful miracles the Lord did through him. Then I came across this remarkable sentence: 'Nothing happened for about three years.' No more miracles. Nothing worthy of note. Simply a time of resting in God, being hidden in a cleft in The Rock.

For the next three years, that was our experience too. At first it appeared as if the Father had forgotten us. But we held on to each other – and to God. God tested us to strengthen us, and made this period a foundation on which to build a stronger faith in Him.

I started to write again – some short stories and articles for magazines. One day an editor suggested I ought to write a book.

'About what?' I asked.

'You,' he replied. 'Your testimony.'

'But it's not complete yet. Who wants to read half a story?'

The editor laughed.

'What's wrong with an interim report? Tell people what God has done in your life so far.'

I liked the idea. I had time, and needed to pause and consider all that God had already done in me. This seemed as good a time as any. I began work, still wondering what God was going to do with us next.

One morning, light broke through once more . . .

I woke up that morning with a start. I had dreamt of a man who was pleading, 'Come and help us!' His name, and even his address, were etched on my mind. At first I thought the Lord was leading me to someone who was sick and needing healing.

I shared the dream with Jan, and told her I intended to write to this man.

'You can't do that!' Jan said. 'You can't just write to people you don't know. Anyway he might not even exist!'

'If he's sick, and the Lord is sending me, I must,' I replied. 'His name is Brian Andrew Barnett, and he lives at Bushey Heath. That won't be difficult to check.'

I found Bushey Heath on the map, but I was a little disappointed. On my map Bushey Heath was all one word, while in my dream it had definitely been two separate words.

'I like my visions to be exact in every detail,' I told Jan.

That morning I wrote to Brian Barnett, telling him about myself and asking who he was and was he in some need. Jan still thought I was mad to do it but, as always, let me go ahead and do what I thought right.

A day or so later Brian Barnett telephoned. It seemed he was not sick, but a state overseer for the Church of God, a worldwide Pentecostal church with headquarters in Cleveland, Tennessee, U.S.A.

Brian was very enthusiastic. I related to him some of the things that God had been doing in our lives, and the reason for my letter. Brian mentioned that he was looking for men with ministerial training and experience to head new churches in England.

We agreed to get together and discuss the situation further. Jan and I rejoiced in the Lord, but hoped that Brian would not ask us to start a new church in Peterborough. We didn't like the city, and desperately wanted to move somewhere else. On top of that, several other ministers had tried to start new churches in the area and failed. How could I succeed if they, more experienced men, had not?

When Brian visited us, we shared with him our fears, and agreed that if God was calling us elsewhere He would make it plain. If not, then He would accomplish His purpose in this area despite the seeming impossibility.

Jan and I spent the next few days in prayer and fasting. The Lord gave both of us a real assurance that Peterborough was His place for us and that He would do great things through us once more.

'Well, Lord,' I told Him, 'no one else but You can do it. The people in this town need to see you as they have never seen you before. You've done it before, now Lord, do it again!'

Our three years of resting in Him were over. Now it was time to start working with Him again.

Chapter Fifteen

Home Ground

The start of our work in Peterborough was blessed by the Lord even more than we could have imagined.

I began with a house-to-house survey to find out what I was up against. How were people going to respond to the idea of a Pentecostal church in their area?

In fact there was an encouraging amount of interest, and twenty-eight people attended our very first service – all of them non-Christians. Six made a profession of faith.

Over the next three weeks attendance averaged twenty-five and several people were healed. On the second Sunday a man was healed of partial blindness, and later two more people were healed: a woman with severe arthritis and another who had been paralysed for nine years following a road accident. The love of the Lord filled the church, and His people responded in worship.

Miracles continue. A young girl about to go on a kidney machine was instantly healed of her kidney disease, and her mother was healed of a serious heart disease at the same time.

Miracles continue – but they began with a miracle in me. When I look back and consider all that the Lord has done in me thus far, I can think of only one word adequate enough to describe it – Hallelujah!

Of all the places where I have testified and preached, the one that stands out is Sheffield.

Although I had visited and been reconciled to my parents after my conversion, and witnessed to them on several occasions, there had been no clear response from them to the gospel. Both Father and Mother were thrilled and impressed with what God had done in me, and with my life, and let me know how proud they were of me, but when I tried to nail them down to the demands of the gospel for them personally, they retreated.

'It's no good,' I moaned to Jan. 'They're too hardened in sin.'

'Rubbish!' Jan cut me short. 'Don't you think people must have thought that about you, once?'

I had to agree. If God could save me, He could save anyone – even my family who had never given any thought to God in their entire lives.

'Right!' I enthused. 'What they need is a big crusade in Sheffield.'

'Whoa!' Jan laughed. 'Who are you to tell God what they need? Let's pray it through first and see what He thinks.'

So we prayed. And the more I prayed, the more I was convinced that the only way my parents could be reached with the gospel was at a crusade. However, I wasn't happy about organising a city-wide crusade just for my parents.

'Well, if God really wants a crusade in Sheffield let Him organise it for you,' Jan said. 'Then you'll know it's His will, and not yours.'

I agreed. The Lord had used Jan many times in the past both to stop me running ahead of Him, and to speed me up when I lagged behind. Now, I started praying in earnest. One night I dreamed I was preaching to a huge congregation. The place was the Town Hall in Sheffield. On the front row sat Father, Mother, and my sister. There were many healings that night among the 2,000 or so people there, and when I made an appeal for people to receive Jesus Christ as their personal Saviour both my parents and my sister raised their hands.

I awoke rejoicing, and related the dream to Jan. As soon

as I had finished telling Jan, the telephone rang. It was 7.30 a.m. and I couldn't imagine who would be calling at that time in the morning.

'Is that Reverend John Bailey?' a strange voice enquired. I said, 'Yes.'

'Sorry to ring so early, but we are planning a city-wide crusade at Sheffield Town Hall and wondered if you could come up to speak?'

It was the minister of the local Pentecostal church in Sheffield. After saying I should like very much to speak at the crusade, Jan and I danced round the room praising the Lord.

The next time I visited my parents I invited them to come and hear me speak. They agreed enthusiastically, and even promised to bring their neighbours.

Sheffield Town Hall was full when I stood up to speak. Father, Mother, my sister and their friends were all sitting on the front row. We had a wonderful time of praise and worship, and many people were healed. Then, as I stood up to speak, I looked at my family and the Lord filled my heart with real love for them. As simply as I could I told them the story of the Prodigal Son and how it related to my life. Mother and my sister were soon in tears, and I could see Father's mouth twitching with emotion.

I believe I spoke as I had never spoken before. The Lord anointed my words and I had the joy of leading my sister to the Lord. Although Mother was less vocal, God touched her, and she told me later that she had started to pray and read the Bible every day.

'What about Father?' I asked.

Mother nodded.

'He isn't ready to say yet,' she said. 'But God spoke to him in that meeting – give him time.'

I know that God will soon complete the work He has begun in their lives, even as He did in mine – Glory to His Name!

This story is far from complete, it is simply an 'interim report' of what the Lord has done thus far. I see a great deal that the Lord has yet to do in me, but I praise Him for what He has already accomplished. These last ten years since I gave my heart to Him seem almost unbelievable.

Sometimes I catch myself wondering if it is all a dream and I'll wake up back on Piccadilly with a syringe in my hand . . .

But, no! With God the impossible is possible. He makes the dream reality, and makes the rebel a priest and a king.

Afterword

The doctor nodded and told me to get dressed.

'Am I fit, then, Doctor?'

The doctor looked at his notes again.

'You are forty years old?' he asked.

I nodded. The doctor shrugged his shoulders.

'You are as fit as a twenty-year-old, and from what you've told me, it's a miracle!'

'Thank you, Doctor,' I grinned. 'And you are right. It is a miracle.'

At the age of twenty, I looked and felt like a forty-year-old. Now, at forty, I was as fit as a twenty-year-old. The Lord has a keen sense of humour – and restores to us the years the wild locusts have eaten.

Why on earth – or in Heaven – God loved me so much that He sent His own Son to die for me, only He knows. But this I do know, it wasn't because of anything in me. It was '. . . his glorious grace which he freely bestowed . . .' on me.

> For consider your call, brethren; not many of you were wise according to worldly standards, not many were powerful, not many were of noble birth; but God chose what is foolish in the world to shame the wise, God chose what is weak in the world to shame the strong, God chose what is low and despised in the world, even things that

are not, to bring to nothing things that are, so that no human being might boast in the presence of God (1 Cor. 1 : 26–9).

I believe that we are in the last days. All around the world there are signs that Christians are rediscovering the power of God. The sick are being healed as an integral part of the proclamation of the gospel – and not merely by the 'gifted' few. God is using people like me and you.

Jesus did not choose 'great' men to be His disciples. He chose twelve men, not only representatives of the twelve tribes of Israel, but who also typified all men. Jesus knew each man – and all men – better than they knew themselves – or we, ourselves – and He chose them because He saw in them all mankind.

Jesus knew their faults, and their potential. He chose them because they were exactly like you and me. Never say that you are too marred to be used by God – see your counterpart among the twelve.

One of them betrayed Jesus, another denied all knowledge of Him, and finally they all deserted Him. Yet Jesus did not forsake them. He did not reject them, or choose twelve others. In their hour of need, Jesus met them on the road to Emmaus, and in the upper room (Luke 24: 13–53).

The question is not 'Are you qualified?' but 'Are you called?' Do you have a personal relationship with the Lord Jesus Christ? If you have, then you are called.

The power to live a victorious Christian life is given not as a 'reward' for holiness, or as a 'sign' of spirituality, but because of need. Jesus said:

If any one thirst, let him come to me and drink. He who believes in me, as the scripture has said, 'Out of his heart shall flow rivers of living water.' Now this he said about the Spirit, which those who believed in him were to receive; for as yet the Spirit had not been given, because Jesus was not yet glorified (John 7 : 37–9).

If you are aware of a lack in your Christian experience – and I am speaking about actual experience, not your doctrinal position – then confess your need by *asking* the

Father to pour out on you the promised Holy Spirit as He did upon the first Christians. Next, *believe* that He *has*, according to His promise to those who ask (Luke 11 : 13). Finally, *receive* the Holy Spirit by faith, and the experience will surely follow: 'Therefore I tell you, whatever you *ask* in prayer, *believe* that you *receive* it, and you *will*' (Mark 11 : 24).

One of the greatest lessons I have learned is that God will never compel any of His children to be more victorious, effective, or dynamic than they want to be.

'God's gifts,' said Meister Eckhart '. . . are meted out according to the taker, not according to the giver.' If we enjoyed God's gifts according to the giver there would be no spiritual or material poverty among us, for there is no lack in God.

A. W. Tozer, in his book *That Incredible Christian*, gives four propositions it would be profitable for every Christian to meditate upon. They are:

1. *You will get nothing unless you go after it.* God has promised to give, but He gives us the responsibility to claim it '. . . every place that the sole of your foot will tread upon I have given to you' (Josh 1 : 3).

2. *You may have as much as you insist upon having.* God delights in Holy boldness in His people, but hates lukewarmness. '. . . yet because of his importunity he will . . . give him whatever he needs' (Luke 11 :8).

3. *You will have as little as you are satisfied with.* The Christian who is satisfied with a joyless, barren life will never experience the joy of the Holy Spirit or the deep satisfaction of fruitful and abundant living. '. . . you do not have, because you do not ask . . .' (Jas. 4 : 2).

4. *You now have as much as you really want.* You are now as victorious and effective as you want to be. You have only yourself to blame if you have settled for something less than God wants for you. He has given us free will. God never uses His omnipotence to make us more victorious and effective than we want to be.

Our asking, however great, is always limited. And our boldest request makes only the smallest demand on God's infinite capacity to give. Would that we ignore the opinions of men and storm God's treasure house, and then plead with God to increase our capacity to receive!

If you have found this book helpful, or if I can help you further, please write to:

Rev. John Bailey
2 Artindale
South Bretton
Peterborough
Cambs PE 3 6YL
England.